Amazing Ageing

... or how to grow into freedom and contentment

**The psychological survival manual for those
approaching older age**

"Better than Botox, cheaper than cosmetic surgery"

David Buswell

Paperback ISBN 978-1-78092-467-0
ePub ISBN 978-1-78092-468-7
PDF ISBN 978-1-78092-469-4

Published in the UK by MX Publishing
335 Princess Park Manor, Royal Drive, London, N11 3GX

www.mxpublishing.co.uk   (UK & Europe)

www.mxpublishing.com (USA)

Cover design by www.staunch.com

With love and thanks to the 4Rs (in alpha order):

Rachel Alexander

Rona Buswell

Ruth Pimenta

Riaz Rhemtulla

Contents

Appendices I

Why I am writing this book

Life is difficult.[1] Living is difficult, ageing is difficult. We grow old from the day we are born. This is an obvious but overlooked truth. Overlooked, because often we dare not, cannot, look at our ageing; will not bring ourselves to stare it fully in the face. At some point the mirror begins to reflect back to us the truth that the face into which we stare is older, the flesh is less firm, the eyes less bright; the body is less supple, the spine more bent, the pull is downwards, earthwards. As the body breaks down and becomes stiffer and less flexible, we become more rigid and more frozen in our thinking and behaviour; there is a tendency to become stuck in the past, clinging to outmoded values and beliefs while rejecting newness, change and difference.

I am writing this book for people like me who want to age amazingly; who want life to be easier rather than more difficult with the passing years. Getting older is unknown territory. People have done it before and will carry on doing it; more and more people are doing it every day - the 2011 Census showed that 9.2 million people in England & Wales are aged over 65 (an increase of more than 10 per cent since 2001); the number of people aged over 90 rose by more than a quarter over the same period; the number over 100 rose by two-thirds. Getting older may be a voyage into uncharted waters, but a lot more people are doing it, and you are doing it right now.

Ageing is an inevitable, day by day, step by step process which is so gradual it is rare for us to stop and notice the changes which are occurring. Once in a while something will occur which brings us up sharp - we meet friends we have not seen for years and think 'They've aged', or something mechanical suddenly or gradually works less well or seizes up and this reminds us that life is impermanent and constantly changing.

---

[1] These three words are the first sentence of *The Road Less Travelled,* M Scott Peck. I have lifted them wholesale because they reflect the experience of many.

1

Given that ageing happens to all of us throughout life, it is curious the bookshelves sag and the internet groans under the weight of lifestyle manuals, fitness bibles and health-&-beauty handbooks; all with the worthy intention of holding back the demonic triplets of decay, decline and deterioration. To wage war on physical ageing is akin to attempting to hold back the sea; the opposing forces are invincible and the waves keep rolling in. And yet so little has been written about ageing well or amazingly. While the focus on how to slow physical ageing has its place, I strongly believe that the greatest return on your investment of time and effort will come from working on the 'inner you'. The 'outer you' will inevitably grow older, develop cracks, break down at inconvenient moments and ultimately let you down; the 'inner you' is where growth can occur, it is where you can refresh, revitalise and re-energise yourself certain in the knowledge that the 'inner you' does not age or fall apart.

I want to age in a way that is as positive as possible - not just in terms of what I eat or drink, or how much I exercise ; I want my transition into older age to be packed full with the green shoots and lush foliage of inner growth: I do not want to shrink or shrivel up mentally, emotionally and spiritually. My hunch is that if I grow inside, it will be reflected on the outside. It is my wish and my intention that I be happy, content, positive and accepting of the inevitable outer changes which will come. And, at the last, I want to leave this life knowing that I have done the best I could, passing, depending on your belief system, into oblivion, the heavenly after-life or the next reincarnation gratefully and without regrets.

This is not a book about dying; it is a book about living. As Wittgenstein[2] wrote "Death is not an event in life; we do not live to experience death." It is not a book about doing, but about being. It is not a book about the external, the outer you, but about the inner you.

---

[2] From Tractatus Logico-Philosophicus, Routledge, 2 edition, 2001. ISBN-13: 978-0415254083

Why this book is for you

My invitation to you is to read this book because it will offer you the choice of ageing in a way which is amazing! I acknowledge wholeheartedly my debt to *The Warmth Of The Heart Prevents Your Body From Rusting* by Marie de Hennezel[3] which is described, rightly, as a meditation on ageing. I wanted to go further, much further, and not just think about ageing, but to explore and discover what can be done about it and, crucially, how to do it.

Few are they who welcome ageing with open arms and a thankful heart; many are they who approach the foothills in fear and trembling of the terrain that lies ahead. Put starkly, we have a choice between a dismal, bitter, sad old age, or an amazing, uplifting and tranquil journey to the end. Admittedly, this is a blatantly black and white view of the world, but then why would you choose to live at the dark, negative end of the spectrum when you could be at the bright, light and optimistic end? What sort of ageing do you choose for yourself – negative or optimistic; awful or amazing? Do you choose to be swamped by the fears, the losses, the sadness of ageing; or to take the opportunity to adapt, change and grow? You do have a choice. You always have a choice.

The aim of this book is to open up for you the range of choices available. My wish is, as you grow older, to enable you to live in a state of grateful acceptance, to help you to develop an attitude which uses these years as a time of inner growth.

I am in my sixties - it might be said I am on the nursery slopes of ageing - and my experience of it is limited, but I know people who are on the Cresta Run. I have drawn on their experience and wisdom. I have dug into my knowledge and experience of Buddhism, on a transpersonal therapy known as

---

[3] de Hennezel, M. (2011) *The Warmth Of The Heart Prevents Your Body From Rusting,* London: Rodale

Psychosynthesis[4] and on the techniques of Neuro Linguistic Programming [5] (NLP) - all of which have the power to effect significant change by widening the range of choices open to us moment by moment.

Buddhism, Psychosynthesis and NLP. Some of the discussion - the parts that challenge your existing mode of thinking and suggest new ways - are based on Buddhist teachings. Most of the exercises – the 'how to do it' sections that guide you through the translation of what you have learned into reality – come from Psychosynthesis and NLP. So why these three?

- Buddhism is a way of life, a way of thinking and a way of living. It is but one way, not <u>the</u> way; nor is it a religion, although it has elements in common with other religions (a moral code, for example). The Buddha's teachings deal with reality and truths that can be verified by personal experience - you can read the words, test them out and incorporate them into everyday living.

- Psychosynthesis is but one form of personal development. It aims to synthesise the many different (and sometimes conflicting) parts of our personality, to harmoniously integrate, for example, those parts of us that are loving, critical, peaceful, aggressive, sensible and foolish in a holistic way, such that we evolve to achieve our highest potential. Psychosynthesis is inclusive insofar as no part of us, however magnificent or however appalling, is excluded; the light is as much a part of us as the shadow. It is accepting; acknowledging not only the light, the dark, and the grey cloudy bits in between, but also it lifts us up so that we can see and move towards the sun of our unrealised potential rising over the distant hills. Psychosynthesis recognises in

---

[4] A description of Psychosynthesis is given at Appendix B
[5] A description of Neuro Linguistic Programming is to be found at Appendix C

4

each of us an impulse to wholeness and supports and nurtures this.

- Neuro Linguistic Programming identifies patterns of thinking and, where change is desired, employs a range of approaches and exercises to affect this change. Whereas Psychosynthesis is spiritual and mystical, NLP is practical and hands-on. The 'problem' is identified, the technique is applied, the change is tested to ensure it is robust and reliable. It is very powerful.

If you are new to such approaches - Buddhism, Psychosynthesis and NLP - you may, at first, find them unfamiliar and perhaps even a little 'way out'; my advice is to persist in spite of your discomfort because it will lessen considerably and the outcome will be worth the effort. Read with an open mind. Give the exercises a go (remembering that they are not compulsory!); the first one you do may not go exactly to plan, but, no matter, try it again, or move on to another one, or skip to the next section.

The exercises have the ability to loosen up rigid ways of thinking, feeling and behaving; they can bring ease and comfort where there is pain and distress; they can help you to collaborate contentedly with the inevitable. Two bits of advice on doing the exercises. Some of them require you to close your eyes which means you cannot read the exercise! I suggest you read it into a voice recorder before you do it. Second, some of the approaches may be unfamiliar to you; I recommend you give the exercise a go and, if you feel you are unsuccessful, that you return to it later.

I invite you to read this book because it is part handbook (the 'what to do') and part guidebook (the 'how to do it') to take with you on your journey into the rest of your life.

1.
The Three Parts Of You

You will be almost certainly be familiar with the age old concept of Body, Mind and Spirit - your physical body, your inner you and your soul.

Your physical body is the container of your personality. Your inner you includes your conscious and unconscious processes and acts as your central controller. Your soul is the you that is beyond personality.

Your physical body, the outer you, is the mechanical bit - your arms and legs, your hands and feet, your face, your hair and skin – as well as the parts you cannot see such as your internal organs – bones, heart, veins, lungs, liver, kidneys etc. Your body is the vehicle of the inner you and it translates your thoughts, feelings and impulses into behaviour and action. It is subject to great change as you grow from your biological formation in the womb, pop out into the world as a bouncing baby, develop into adolescence, expand into maturity and then move into old age, and finally die. Your physical body is visible and mechanical. The process of ageing is apparent through the progressively more defective mechanism; the plumbing furs up and the internal wiring breaks down. Like an elderly car, your body won't start on cold mornings, breaks down unexpectedly, and develops leaks!

The inner you is that part of you which directly experiences your thoughts, your feelings and sensations. Note that your inner you _experiences_ your thoughts, feelings and sensations – it is _not_ your thoughts, feelings and sensations. Your inner you is separate from thinking and feeling and this separation gives you control, if you choose, over your mind and emotions. In the Western world this separateness is not often acknowledged and as Roberto Assagioli[6] said: "(This is) a

---

[6] Roberto Assagioli (b Venice, February 27, 1888 d Capolona d'Arezzo, August 23, 1974) was an Italian psychiatrist much interested in

fundamental psychological principle. We are dominated by everything with which our self is identified. We can dominate and control everything from which we disidentify (separate) ourselves. Some people get their identity from their feelings, others from their thoughts..."[7] Some, however, get their identity from their physical body; for people who are strongly identified with their physical body, ageing can be difficult and frightening.

Your inner you is not the plaything of your feelings and emotions but has the capacity to be their master. You can become the conductor of your own orchestra, in control of the vast instrumental forces which, left to themselves, would produce a cacophonous, discordant din. The development and synthesis of your inner you allows you to become the puppet master – you are no longer the puppet. You pull your own strings.

The inner you changes as you develop and mature. From birth to about age five[8] your focus is on your physical body as you learn the basics of survival, movement, infant sexuality and control; during the rest of the first decade your focus is still on your body and the subtleties of coordination and movement, but you are beginning to have feelings of guilt and shame; in adolescence, strong feelings, raw and undefined, move into the foreground as you experience love, hate, righteous indignation and, at the same time, search for personal identity and meaning to understand who you are and where in the world you fit. Assuming that you were brought up in a supportive, nurturing environment, you will begin to establish a sense of identity and your body, feelings and mind become integrated into a balanced personality. If you didn't grow up in a nurturing home, your

---

humanistic and transpersonal psychology. He created the psychological movement known as Psychosynthesis; an approach which regards a person as having a personality and being a Soul. More detail about Psychosynthesis is given in Appendix B.

[7] Keen, S. *The Golden Mean of Roberto Assagioli*. Psychology Today. December 1974

[8] Adapted from a training seminar given by Tom Yeomans at the Psychosynthesis Institute, California in 1978 and summarised in The Unfolding Self by Molly Young Brown (1983)

identity may be fragmented and your personality split. During your thirties you develop a sense of purpose, your values become clearer but less rigid; in your forties and fifties you begin to explore meaning and purpose more widely as energies which are beyond consciousness are triggered – these years can be times of existential crisis when you begin to question what life is all about, what is missing and whether this is all there is. Bob Geldof's book *Is That It?* was a pertinent title for a book by a man in his 40s!. Then comes the obdurate onset of ageing, a time during which you will reflect on the mysteries of life as your soul begins to express itself more fully through your personality.

Your inner you also contains your mind, or, to be more accurate your two minds – your conscious and your unconscious mind. In the context of this book and the exercises and techniques I will be using to help you grow as you age, the unconscious mind will be more in the foreground than the conscious. I have included a brief discussion of the unconscious mind and its importance in Appendix A.

The third part of you is your soul, sometimes called your Higher Self. If this language is anathema to you because of its religious overtones, please wait one moment before pressing your mental and emotional OFF switch ... and read on. For me, the concept of soul is free of religious association and connotation. No one doctrine has the right to claim that its understanding and interpretation of the soul is the truth; it isn't. At best it is a considered rationalisation of one of life's mysteries.

My thinking (and this view is a belief; it is not the truth!) is that my soul is that part of me which is a source of wisdom and guidance; it is the essence of me, is outside of my body and is eternal. This is what I mean by soul and when in the course of this book I make mention of "your soul", it is shorthand for saying "your eternal source of wisdom and guidance".

Personally I find the concept of the soul very persuasive because it:

8

- Hypothesises a dimension of myself which is beyond body and personality;
- Suggests limitless potential and possibility;
- Is the locus of my spiritual being;
- Is constant, unchanging and enduring;
- Is the home of the real me.

The Indian mystic, Sathya Sai Baba[9] said that "We are three people, the person we think we are, the person others think we are, and the person we really are." The person you really are is the part of you that is connected to and tuned in to your soul. Your soul is a resource of advice and support to your inner you. Your soul and your inner you are separate but connected.

This is a simple model with three component parts – physical you, inner you and soul. For me it is a model which works, is simple and has practical positive application. These parts are interconnected and a change in one part will have an impact on the other parts.

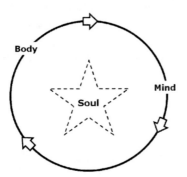

If you work on your inner you, it will bring about change in your physical body (but not your soul, which is constant and unchanging). It has been demonstrated that older people who

[9] Quotation taken from "Dr. Harvey and Dr. Goldstein Region 5 Visit - Feb. 20, 2000" which is to be found at:
http://www.saibaba.ws/articles/harveygoldstein.htm

are happier live longer, with less disability and stay physically fit longer into old age.[10]

The physical body is not within the scope of this book. There are shelves of books, pages on the internet, lifestyle magazines, TV programmes – all bursting with articles and advice on diet, exercise, how to maintain a vigorous sex life while perfecting your golf swing, looking younger, the invigorating properties of seaweed, etc. There are doctors, alternative therapists, yoga or Pilates classes, health spas, Botox, beauty treatments enough without me swelling the tide.

Your inner you, your personality, is not visible to others (except insofar as it manifests in your behaviour) and is capable of change. The inner you is capable of growth even while your physical body is deteriorating. This is the joy of the inner you – that you are able to take control of what you think, what you feel and how you behave, and you can make changes if you choose.

Your soul is unchanging and eternal. It is the rock in the shifting sand, the lighthouse in the swirling sea. As the shadows of your life lengthen and your body begins to lose its sheen, you can rest on the rock and be guided home by the light.

As the outer diminishes, the inner can grow.

---

[10] From *The Dynamics of Ageing: Evidence from the ENGLISH LONGITUDINAL STUDY OF AGEING 2002-10 (Wave 5)*. Editors: James Banks, James Nazroo, Andrew Steptoe The full findings of the research can be found at www.ifs.org.uk/ELSA

2.
The challenges of ageing

I started this book with three words "Life is difficult." It is. And it is all too easy to paint a grim and miserable picture of an appalling and frightening physical, mental and emotional decline such as Larkin suggests in *Old Fools*:

> *"What do they think has happened, the old fools,*
> *To make them like this? Do they somehow suppose*
> *It's more grown-up when your mouth hangs open and drools,*
> *And you keep on pissing yourself, and can't remember*
> *Who called this morning? Or that, if they only chose,*
> *They could alter things back to when they danced all night,*
> *Or went to their wedding, or sloped arms some September?"[11]*

Ageing is inevitable, unavoidable and inescapable, and it does not have to be horrendous or horrifying. Ageing can be amazing! Look around you and you will see some truly amazing people who are living full and enriching lives without regard for their age. Be inspired by these four examples:

Alice Herz-Sommer (born 1903) trained as a pianist at the Prague Conservatory, married in the early 1930s and had one son, Raphael, a cellist who died at the age of 64. Her story is remarkable for the fact that mother and son survived two years in Terezin (also known as Theresienstadt) concentration camp. While incarcerated Alice played over 100 concerts in the camp; her husband meanwhile had been sent to Auschwitz and later died in Dachau. Liberated from Terezin in 1945 she moved to Israel and in 1986 to London where she now has her home. She ascribes her longevity to her optimism. In a

---

[11] *The Old Fools*, Philip Larkin, Collected Poems, Faber & Faber, London, 1988, p196

BBC programme on centenarians, Mrs Herz-Sommer said "My twin sister was a terrible pessimist, she died when she was not yet 70 because she never laughed, never. Laughing is beautiful though.... I am an optimist, for me it's only the good things, never a bad thought". [12]

David Attenborough (born 1926) continues to create documentaries about life on our planet with energetic enthusiasm and erudition. He has been at the forefront of bringing high quality, beautifully crafted productions like *Life On Earth*, *The Living Planet*, *The Trials Of Life*, *The Private Life Of Plants* and *First Life* to audiences around the globe. He is a passionate supporter of environmental causes, has highlighted the case of a prisoner of conscience, collaborated on musicals and appeared in *The Last Night Of The Proms.*

In 2003, Ranulph Fiennes (born 1944) undertook seven marathons in seven days on seven continents in the Land Rover 7x7x7 Challenge for the British Heart Foundation; this in spite of having recently suffered a heart attack and having a double heart bypass only a few months earlier. In 2007, he climbed the north face of the Eiger even though he had a fear of heights; in 2009 he climbed to the summit of Everest, not only becoming the oldest British person so to do, but achieving the distinction of being the first person ever to have climbed Everest and crossed the ice caps of the north and south poles.

Prince Philip, Duke of Edinburgh, (born 1921) is husband to Queen Elizabeth II (born 1926), in which capacity he has become the oldest spouse ever of a reigning British monarch. He is an energetic enthusiast, patron of scores of organisations, founder of the Duke of Edinburgh's Award, and Chancellor of Cambridge University. He played polo until he was 50, at which point he began to compete in carriage driving. He has been a yachtsman

[12] http://m.bbc.co.uk/news/magazine-18613263

and is an experienced pilot (by the time he was 70 he had built up over 5,000 flying hours). He paints in oils and collects art. Prince Philip has a direct and uncompromising personality, his gaffes are legendary and he has been described as HRH Victor Meldrew[13].

This is what Joan Bakewell and Penelope Lively have to say about ageing:

> "I think there are many reasons to be happy as you get older. Life's battles have been fought and either won or lost and it's too late for regret. So you're not fighting old battles. Jealousy is inappropriate, ambition is over; it's too late. So there are lots of discards, there are a lot of things you can do without. And that clears the ground for a lot of pleasures in life – simple pleasures and really quite profound pleasures." [14]

> "... one of the odd things about old age, when it has stalked and seized you (and however did this come about?) is that you find you have this new power of accommodation ....There is a certain carefree element to old age, I find; you are beyond wanting to impress, to leave a mark. Ambition - what was that? Aspiration is still around; I would still like to write a good book." [15]

For many, and I think for women more than for men, the biggest ordeal is the outward, inexorable physical changes as *"the bits that were you / start speeding away from each other"* (Larkin again[16]). Cosmetic surgery comes at a price which is not just financial since while it may delay the outward signs of physical ageing, there are risks attached (remember the faulty

---

[13] Victor Meldrew is a perpetually discontented and grumpy old man (in his sixties) from a BBC situation comedy *One Foot In The Grave*.
[14] Interview with Dame Joan Bakewell by Anita Singh *Don't worry, life gets better once you pass 70,* Daily Telegraph, April 9th 2012
[15] *We oldies are the new kids on the block,* Penelope Lively. Daily Telegraph, July 17th 2012.
[16] *The Old Fools*, Philip Larkin, Collected Poems, Faber & Faber, London, 1988, p196

breast implants scandal of 2012[17]) and unintended consequences such as the appearance of being permanently surprised.

Let's look at some of the other challenges you may face so that they come into your conscious awareness – once you know what dragons may seek to devour you, the better equipped you can be to prepare your response.

1. Suffering: Whatever you become attached to causes you suffering.

"Attachment is the origin, the root of suffering; hence it is the cause of suffering." [18]

Clinging or hanging on causes you suffering. Consider Annie who remains in the family home years after her husband has died and her three children have left. The house is shabby and old-fashioned, the kitchen and bathroom are unchanged since she and William moved in forty years ago, the boiler is inefficient but to replace it would be unthinkably costly, the doors and windows ill-fitting and draughty, the garden, once her greatest pleasure, wild and overgrown. But still she hangs on in this cold, uncomfortable, expensive and unmanageable house. Why? Because it is full of distorted and exaggerated memories of a life that is now over - of children playing on the lawn, of singing carols round the tree in the hall, of cooking family meals on the Aga. To move would be inconceivable, to stay is unbearable.

Attachment to goods and chattels are not the only things which cause you to suffer by a refusal to let them go and take their rightful place in your personal

---

[17] In the UK an estimated 47,000 women were thought to have breast implants manufactured by the French company Poly Implant Prothese (PIP), which were filled with industrial grade silicone. PIP sold 300,000 implants worldwide.
[18] The Dalai Lama at Harvard, 1988, Snow Lion USA, p.37

history book – you may have memories of past times, thoughts and feelings which are now redundant and which could be ditched or updated. Hanging on to them causes suffering. In your life it may be time to let go of the past and to move into the present, to give up fighting the old battles, to allow ambition to go on its way, to wave farewell to regrets, repressed emotions, remorse, guilt, past traditions and pretentions, to stop hanging on to any desire for social approval. Time to thaw the parts of you that are frozen and to unlock the parts that are sealed and closed off.

And time too to be aware that not all of life is about suffering. There are wonders all around. Blue skies, birds, babies, rain, waterfalls, the seashore, sunrise and sunset, the moon and the stars.

2. Loss: As you age, the losses multiply. Which of these losses have you experienced?

- Death of loved ones
- Friends
- Work
- Role
- Status or position
- Usefulness
- Power
- Ambition
- Control
- Independence
- Flexibility
- Looks
- Body image
- Hair
- A limb
- Memory
- Cognitive sharpness
- Health
- Energy / vitality
- Humour

Brenda's husband, Victor, died three years ago at the age of 74, shortly after they had celebrated their golden wedding anniversary. He remains her central point of reference and her decreasing number of friends have long tired of Vic and the extent to which Brenda continues to feel her loss. Vic features in all her conversation. When her drains were blocked and she had to call a plumber, she told the poor man several times what Vic would have done. His opinion is quoted on matters of which, during his life, he would have been indifferent or ignorant - the state of the economy, young people today, the ineffectiveness of the government, etc.

3. Regrets: Regretting what you have done or not done, chewing over the opportunities missed or the misfortunes which might have been avoided are other ways in which you can be the author of your own suffering as you grow older. Colin regretted for years that he divorced Zelda who, although 'difficult', he had loved. Now, fifty years on, he ruminates over her almost daily, regretting on the one hand that he did not get help with her drinking, did not confront her infidelity and on the other that he was too hard on her and did not show her compassion.

Bronnie Ware[19], a palliative care nurse, in an article which was widely published in 2012, found that at the time of death there were five common regrets:

> "For many years I worked in palliative care. My patients were those who had gone home to die. Some incredibly special times were shared. I was with them for the last three to twelve weeks of their lives.
>
> People grow a lot when they are faced with their own mortality. I learnt never to underestimate someone's capacity for growth. Some changes were phenomenal. Each experienced a variety of emotions, as expected, denial, fear, anger, remorse, more denial and eventually acceptance. Every single patient found their

---

[19] The article quoted here was in many national newspapers in January 2012. This particular version is from www.ariseindiaforum.org/nurse-reveals-the-top-5-regrets-people-make-on-their-deathbed.

peace before they departed though, every one of them. When questioned about any regrets they had or anything they would do differently, common themes surfaced again and again. Here are the most common five:

1. *I wish I'd had the courage to live a life true to myself, not the life others expected of me.*

This was the most common regret of all. When people realise that their life is almost over and look back clearly on it, it is easy to see how many dreams have gone unfulfilled. Most people had not honoured even a half of their dreams and had to die knowing that it was due to choices they had made, or not made.
It is very important to try and honour at least some of your dreams along the way. From the moment you lose your health it is too late. Health brings a freedom very few realise, until they no longer have it.

2. *I wish I didn't work so hard.*

This came from every male patient that I nursed. They missed their children's youth and their partner's companionship. Women also spoke of this regret. But as most were from an older generation, many of the female patients had not been breadwinners. All of the men I nursed deeply regretted spending so much of their lives on the treadmill of a work existence.

By simplifying your lifestyle and making conscious choices along the way, it is possible to not need the income that you think you do. And by creating more space in your life, you become happier and more open to new opportunities, ones more suited to your new lifestyle.

3. *I wish I'd had the courage to express my feelings.*

Many people suppressed their feelings in order to keep peace with others. As a result, they settled for a mediocre existence and never became who they were truly capable of becoming. Many developed illnesses relating to the bitterness and resentment they carried as a result.

We cannot control the reactions of others. However, although people may initially react when you change the way you are by speaking honestly, in the end it raises the relationship to a whole new and healthier level. Either that or it releases the unhealthy relationship from your life. Either way, you win.

4. <u>I wish I had stayed in touch with my friends.</u>

Often they would not truly realise the full benefits of old friends until their dying weeks and it was not always possible to track them down. Many had become so caught up in their own lives that they had let golden friendships slip by over the years. There were many deep regrets about not giving friendships the time and effort that they deserved. Everyone misses their friends when they are dying.

It is common for anyone in a busy lifestyle to let friendships slip. But when you are faced with your approaching death, the physical details of life fall away. People do want to get their financial affairs in order if possible. But it is not money or status that holds the true importance for them. They want to get things in order more for the benefit of those they love. Usually though, they are too ill and weary to ever manage this task. It all comes down to love and relationships in the end. That is all that remains in the final weeks, love and relationships.

5. <u>I wish that I had let myself be happier.</u>

This is a surprisingly common one. Many did not realise until the end that happiness is a choice. They had stayed stuck in old patterns and habits. The so-called 'comfort' of familiarity

18

overflowed into their emotions, as well as their
physical lives. Fear of change had them
pretending to others, and to themselves, that
they were content, while deep within, they
longed to laugh properly and have silliness in
their life again.

When you are on your deathbed, what others
think of you is a long way from your mind. How
wonderful to be able to let go and smile again,
long before you are dying.

Life is a choice. It is YOUR life. Choose
consciously, choose wisely, choose honestly.
Choose happiness."

You have the "capacity for growth" and you can change; you can "let go and smile again", so why wait until the last three to twelve weeks of your life?

4. Redundant values and beliefs: Holding on to values and beliefs which have passed their sell-by date can cause discomfort and, sometimes, anger. One of the values which has taken a battering in recent years is respect. When he was a child, Daniel had been taught that he should always stand up when a woman, including his wife, came into the room; his grandson Ed is disinclined to acknowledge anyone, which maddens Daniel, and Ed regards his grandfather's values as old-fashioned and stupid. Values such as respect, courtesy, politeness, consideration for others and even honesty have declined in importance in recent years. I am not suggesting that you should abandon these values, but rather that you let them loosen their grip on you.

Beliefs you held in the past may no longer be serving you well. The belief that the early bird catches the worm may have had some currency when you were inching your way up the ladder of career and ambition, but is less useful if you are now retired but still forcing

19

yourself out of bed at 6am, the time at which you used to get up in order to leave the house to catch the early train into the city. Other beliefs, especially ones you hold about yourself, can be damaging and limiting. Frank holds the belief that 'nobody loves me'. Originating from being dumped in a pitiless children's home by his mother when he was four, this belief may then have had some foundation, but now after many years' evidence to the contrary, Frank still holds onto it and unconsciously acts it out by isolating himself and avoiding contact with others.

5. Isolation and loneliness: The twin monsters of ageing. Isolation is likely to be the more problematic as ageing can bring immobility and the consequent inability to get out and spend time with others means you can be trapped and cut off from other people, from changing ideas, from newness and novelty, and from the rhythm and flow of life.

Loneliness (see Chapter 14), is not the exclusive domain of the ageing, and can be experienced even when young and fully mobile. It is different from being alone or solitary. Loneliness is thinking or feeling that your social relationships are less satisfying than they should be; that is to say it can (sometimes) be a perception rather than the reality.

Gill, who lives alone in the country without the company of family or friends, is both isolated and, in her own words, 'intensely' lonely. She has impaired mobility, can no longer drive due to her blindness and has always found it difficult to make friends due to her acerbic manner and judgmental attitude. Although she once enjoyed sewing, tapestry work and reading, these interests are now denied her. She is unable to watch TV and relies heavily on the radio. Christmas is spent alone. She is profoundly depressed.

Henry lives in a self-contained flat in his daughter's house in central Birmingham, having moved from Dorset when his wife died. He is not alone and has the company of his daughter and her family and a few friends he has made through the tennis club and bowls, but he is very lonely. This is a thought and it can be changed. Henry could reframe his circumstances in the context of gratitude, being grateful for the company he does have, for the love of his daughter and son-in-law, and for the friends he sees most days.

6. Marginalisation: As an older person there is the challenge of becoming ignored and invisible, of being shunted into a siding away from the mainstream of life. Heads no longer turn in the street, the wolf-whistles have long ceased, your opinion is rarely sought, you are at the front of the queue but the last to be served, you are no longer at the centre of things. Yogic *siddhas* can make themselves invisible through concentration and meditation; somehow, as you get older, you can make your body imperceptible to others without the rigorous training of the *siddhas*!

Harriet, once described as 'the blonde bombshell with the big boobies', finds that men no longer give her a glance. Tom, accustomed to handing out advice unsolicited, discovers that people seem bored as soon as he opens his mouth. Ingrid, her mantelpiece once crowded with invitations and she with scarce an evening free, now stays at home in front of her TV while her younger, married friends dine and party.

7. Time - Too Little, Too Much: Einstein came up with the idea that linear time is superficial. Each minute does not have the same value, it is dependent on the context. If you put your hand on the hotplate of an Aga for a minute, it would seem like an hour; if you spent an hour with a close friend, it would seem like a minute.

Time is fluid. You will have noticed that time rushes by when you are busy or enjoying yourself and crawls when you are idle. As you age, the birthdays come round quicker, but the hours can drag. The time left to do all the undone things is short, but the day can be long. There is both too little time and too much.

Claudia Hammond[20], a psychologist and BBC reporter, has said that "when we are doing something new and interesting, time appears to go more quickly. But when we look back retrospectively, our assessment of time is based on how many new individual memories we built up during that period". The answer is to build up new memories, by doing something new or in a different way whenever possible.

8. Living in the past and dreading the future: As the years drift by there is a temptation to live in the past, to hang on to what is familiar, while at the same time dreading what horrors the future may hold. Living in the past avoids living in the present with the attendant risk that you lose touch with the reality and vitality of the world as it is today.

You will never move forward if you are driving using the rear view mirror or facing backwards! Living in the past is unhealthy for you and boring for those around you. How do you respond when you hear someone say 'When I was at Dunkirk....', 'When the children were at home ....', 'When John/Janet was alive...'?

Live your life one day at a time. The past is over, that moment has gone forever and there is no turning back the clock. The future is now, it is today. The distant future is not worth worrying about.

---

[20] Daily Telegraph, April 21st 2012

9. Rigidity: Rigidity comes from being inflexible. If you live your life by a set of rules drawn up when you were a child or a teenager, it may be time to abandon or rewrite them. Who would be guided by last week's weather forecast when walking in the Lake District? There are no rules written about how you should live, except ones handed to you by others which you have swallowed whole without questioning, or the ones that you choose to impose on yourself.

10. Sex: As you age, sexual potency wanes even if desire remains. Two factors are at work - one is the ageing of the physical body, and the other is psychological.

Physically most males reach their sexual peak at age 17 or 18, thereafter it is a long slow journey down the far side of the mountain, which becomes more noticeable after the age of 30. While it's not uncommon for an 18 year old man to achieve orgasm four to eight times in a 24-hour period, most 30 year olds are happy if they manage once. With ageing, men's erections may be less stiff and the force of ejaculation, and the amount ejaculated, may be less. Older women produce less vaginal lubrication due to reduced oestrogen levels, and arousal leading to orgasm may be slower due to slacker muscle tone; contractions of the uterus during orgasm may become painful.

Psychologically there can be factors which impact upon your sex life, such as marital dissatisfaction, death of a partner, resuming sexual relationships with a new partner after the death of a spouse, dislike of your own – or the other person's – body, financial or other stresses, and false expectations about the effect of ageing on sexuality.

Even though the US nonagenarian comic George Burns once remarked that sex was like "shooting pool with a rope", an ABC News report by Patricia Bloom[21] in 2000 said that "A recent survey of married men and women showed that 87% of married men and 89% of married women in the 60-64 age range are sexually active. Those numbers drop with advancing years, but 29% of men and 25% of women over the age of 80 are still sexually active."

11. Intolerance and Ingratitude: It is unlikely to be true that the world becomes a worse place as you get older. In reality, all that is happening is that the world around you is changing, and it is changing in ways that you may not like and, at the same time, your tolerance for change is reducing.

This intolerance can be accompanied by ingratitude driven by the thought or feeling that there is nothing, or very little, to be grateful for: there is too much traffic, the countryside is being vandalized, there is too much immigration, people no longer have time for each other, the young (the Me Generation) are narcissistic and self-absorbed, the long promised pension has disappointed, and, to compound matters, the country is going to the dogs or to hell in a handcart (choose your own metaphor).

Tolerance for change does diminish with age as does wonderment and gratitude. Like many of the things mentioned in the last eleven sections, intolerance and ingratitude are a choice and can be changed. Intolerance can be transformed into acceptance, and ungratefulness into gratitude.

The good news is that even as you age, life can be good, enjoyable and worthwhile. There are many things you can do to

---

[21] Sex In The Elderly, Patricia Bloom, MD. Mount Sinai-New York University Medical Center, ABC News, March 16, 2000 to be found at: www.globalaging.org/health/us/sexelderly

ensure that you have a happier, more contented, more peaceful and pleasurable old age. In the coming chapters I will be giving you tools with which you can work to change your thinking, your feelings and your behaviour and, thereby, allow yourself greater contentment and comfort.

Amazing Ageing has four cornerstones:

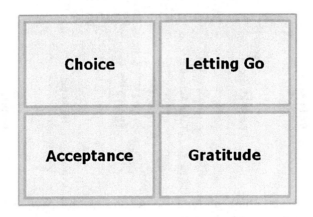

| Choice | Letting Go |
| Acceptance | Gratitude |

Two people set off separately on the journey of their life. One of them has no transport so he travels on foot. He walks round a bend and discovers he is in a cul-de-sac, a choice-block; he retraces his steps and thinks he will turn left and is held back by a letting-go-block; he decides to turn right but it is closed to pedestrians, an acceptance-block; irritated, he spins round on his heels and walks smack into a gratitude block. He is stuck in the place he has always been.

The other has just taken delivery of a new car and is setting off on an adventure all of her own. She makes some basic preparations for her travels. As she goes, she adapts to changing circumstances – road closures, diversions, sudden changes in the weather etc – by making choices carefully and consciously, by letting go of expectations and old ways of thinking, by accepting things as they are, and by being grateful for everything that happens to her. She discovers that the journey is easier than anticipated, that she is enjoying herself and is feeling a sense of freedom.

Amazing Ageing has also six pillars:

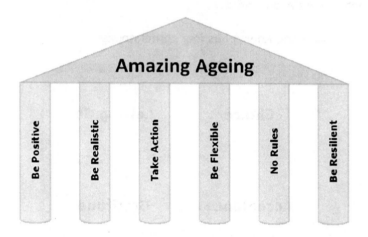

If you think of Amazing Ageing as the new, emerging structure of your life from today onwards, then the cornerstones are its foundation and the six pillars are there to support and strengthen it. Take the first cornerstone – Choice. As you will discover, recognising that you always have a choice whatever your circumstances is essential to Amazing Ageing; having a choice comes alive only if you take action and will be stronger if your choice making has a positive focus, is realistic, is flexible and is not strangled by rules.

Before you begin work on the construction of your Amazing Ageing, you need to do some preparation as you would before undertaking any significant project. First, get yourself a large A4 notebook. Choose with care and buy one which will give you pleasure; you may want to personalise the front cover with photos or drawings because this will be your Journal.

Keeping A Journal

As you develop your inner you, it will greatly aid your understanding of what is unfolding if you keep an "inner" Journal. This is not *Bridget Jones's Diary*, nor an adolescent's diary with its monotonous entries of the 'got up, had breakfast, went out, came home, went to bed' variety. It will be a Journal not about your doings but about your being.

Your inner Journal will track the changing pattern and development of your inner world. In your Journal you can:

- Record your reflections on your relationships, your dreams, your desires and hopes, and your fantasies. You can write here things that you do not have the courage to talk about with other people.

- Log the outcome of the exercises given throughout this book.

- Write down questions you want to ponder later, or jot down insights which come to you.

- Draw pictures to illuminate your thoughts or feelings. Drawing in a semi-conscious way, allowing your hand to do the work, is a wonderful way of accessing your unconscious mind.

- Write the letters you are never going to send. I have written letters in my Journal to friends with whom I am having difficulty, to my parents who although long dead live on in my head. I have written letters to my soul putting forward problems and seeking guidance. Many a time I find that I have written my own answer to the predicament before I have come to the end.

The very act of writing opens up receptivity to insights, not just from within, but from a variety of sources outside of yourself. You may discover that by writing down whatever is troubling you in your Journal you will

27

become open to receiving information or guidance in unexpected ways.

Let's imagine you have written in your Journal about a particular dilemma you are facing; later that day there is something on TV which gives you the solution you were seeking; or you pick up the book you are reading to find words which relate in some way to the issue.

The second piece of preparation is to be clear about where you are starting from.

Where Are You Now?

- Take some crayons or coloured felt tip pens and some paper (or you can use a page of your pristine new Journal!)

- Sit in a comfortable chair and close your eyes.

- Allow your mind to focus softly on where you are in your life and ask yourself 'What is my life like now?'

- Now let your hand draw. Observe with detached curiosity the picture which emerges. Try and avoid judgement - it does not have to be perfect!

- Draw whatever comes. It may be an obvious representation of something or it may be formless, shapeless and fuzzy. Just let your hand (not your head) guide you.

- When you have finished, stand up and dance a little jig. Take a few deep breaths.

- Now look at what you have drawn. What is it saying to you? What feelings does it bring up? Do you feel happy or sad, calm or angry? Is it personal or impersonal? Warm or cold? Is there movement in your drawing or is it static and what might this mean? What stands out for you? Is there anything missing from your drawing and what might this mean?

- Look at it from another angle – turn it sideways or the wrong way up – and ask yourself the same questions.

- Take time to reflect on what this drawing has to say to you about your life now and where you are.

- In your Journal, record your reflections. As you write, other things may bubble up – write them down. This is not for publication so you can let go of the constraints of looking good or pleasing others, and considerations of punctuation, grammar and sense.

The final piece of preparation is to be clear about where you are going. Once you know where you are starting from and where you are heading, you can plan your journey.

Where Are You Going?

- As before, take some crayons or coloured felt tip pens and some paper (or use your Journal).

- Sit in a comfortable chair and close your eyes.

- Allow your mind to focus softly on your vision of your future life and ask yourself 'What will my life be like?'

- Now let your hand draw. Observe with detached curiosity the picture which emerges. Try and avoid judgement or perfectionism.

- Draw whatever comes. It may be an obvious representation of something or it may be formless, shapeless and fuzzy. Just let your hand (not your head) guide you.

- When you have finished, stand up, stretch and dance a little jig. Take a few deep breaths.

- Now look at what you have drawn. What is it saying to you? What feelings does it bring up? Do you feel happy or sad, calm or angry? Is it personal or impersonal?

Warm or cold? Is there movement in your drawing or is it static and what might this mean? What stands out for you? Is there anything missing from your drawing and what might this mean?

- Look at it from another angle – turn it sideways or the wrong way up – and ask yourself the same questions.

- Take time to reflect on what this drawing has to say to you about your future life and where you are going.

- In your Journal, record your reflections. Other thoughts or feelings may bubble up as you write - make a note of them.

Now you know where you are and have an insight to how you view your future. Time for you to be introduced to the four cornerstones of Amazing Ageing.

Amazing Ageing

The Four Cornerstones

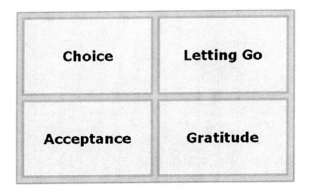

3.
Choice

This is the best news in the book - you have a choice!

I will repeat: **you can choose** and, better still, **you always have a choice.** In the article on the Top Five Regrets of the Dying from which I quoted earlier, Bronnie Ware writes:

- "Most people had not honoured even a half of their dreams and <u>had to die knowing that it was due to choices they had made, or not made</u>."
- "Many did not realise until the end that <u>happiness is a choice</u>. They had stayed stuck in old patterns and habits."
- "<u>Life is a choice. It is YOUR life</u>. Choose consciously, choose wisely, choose honestly. Choose happiness."

Bronnie also wrote that "People grow a lot when they are faced with their own mortality. I learnt never to underestimate someone's capacity for growth". You have the capacity to grow, and to grow now, not leaving it until the last three months of your existence. You can choose life and amazing ageing, or you can choose a sterile moribund future.

I was in my late 40s, training in Psychosynthesis, when I realised for the first time that I had choices, that I always had a choice whatever the situation, and it was the experiences of two remarkable men that brought this home to me most fully:

"We who lived in the concentration camps can remember the men who walked through the huts comforting others, giving away their last piece of bread. They may have been few in number, but they offer sufficient proof that everything can be taken from a man but one thing: the

last of his freedoms – to choose one's attitude in any given set of circumstances, to choose one's own way." [22]

"I realised I was free to take one of many attitudes toward the situation, to give one value or another to it, to utilise it in one way or another. I could rebel inwardly and curse; or I could submit passively, vegetating; or I could indulge in the unwholesome pleasure of self-pity and assume the martyr's role; or I could take the situation in a sporting way and with a sense of humour, considering it as a novel and interesting experience... I could make of it a rest cure or a period of intense thinking, either about personal matters - reviewing my past life and pondering on it - or about scientific and philosophical problems; or I could take advantage of the situation to undertake personal psychological training; or, finally, I could make it into a spiritual retreat. I had the clear, pure perception that this was entirely my own affair; that I was free to choose any or several of these attitudes and activities; that this choice would have unavoidable effects which I could foresee and for which I was fully responsible. There was no doubt in my mind about this essential freedom and power and their inherent privileges and responsibilities" [Roberto Assagioli, 'Freedom in Jail'] [23]

This is extremely powerful; however restricted or limiting your conditions may be, you have the freedom to choose your own way, the freedom to choose any or several attitudes and activities. It means, simply, that you can decide, as you age, who and how you want to be; that at times of crisis, you have a choice in how you respond. However, it is not limitless liberty since you are responsible for your choices.

---

[22] *Man's Search for Meaning*, Viktor Frankl. Beacon Press, 2006, ISBN-13: 978-0-8070-1426-4
[23] Photocopied article from Psychosynthesis & Education Trust, London. Source unknown.

"In the long run, we shape our lives, and we shape ourselves. The process never ends until we die. And the choices we make are ultimately our own responsibility."[24]

You can choose wisely and carefully, or foolishly and carelessly; and whatever you choose you cannot blame anyone else – that is where the self-responsibility comes in. You can elect to make choices which are life-affirming, which focus on the good things that you have and will have in your life and on the gifts and talents you have been given; or you can choose to focus on lack and loss, on how badly off you are and how ill the world has treated you, on the hurts you have suffered and the pains you have endured.

There is no right way, except your way and you are at liberty to choose what that will be. You may not be able to choose how you look, or which parts of your body remain healthy, or which bits of your mind remain robust, but you can choose how you respond to these changes. Why would you not choose the way that will give you the greatest chance of happiness?

You can choose to accept that the 'outer you' will change, that you will no longer have the taut skin, the healthy glow and the perky, pesky sexual impulses you had in your twenties, and you can choose to shift your focus from the outer you to the inner you. This ability to **consciously choose** your response to any challenge – and to do so wisely, carefully, and honestly - will transform your attitude to ageing. You can choose to grow the 'inner you' rather than be miserable as the 'outer you' shrinks and shrivels; you can choose to develop rather than decline; you can choose to 'be' more, rather than to 'do' more.

It is your choice – and this is a heavy responsibility and yours alone – whether you wage an unwinnable war or you move into the next stage of your life calmly and peacefully. At times of pain, crisis or failure, you are offered your greatest

---
[24] From Foreword to *You Learn By Living,* Eleanor Roosevelt, Westminster John Knox Press, 1960

opportunities for growth; you can choose to embrace the discomfort, accepting things exactly as they are, collaborating with the inevitable, blessing whatever obstacles are dropped in your path and using the pain, the crisis or the failure as a stepping stone to growth.

You can 'choose your own way' in how you think or feel. Do you choose to hang on to old ways of thinking, to outmoded values and beliefs, or to let them go? Do you really want to move forwards in your life encumbered with the heavy baggage of regrets, grudges and recriminations, or to dance freely round life's ballroom accepting your past, your faults and failings? At the age of 70 do you still want to be hanging on to the acidity of the acrimonious divorce which happened thirty years previous? Resenting the promotion or salary increase you didn't get? Bemoaning the poor advice you once took about your investments? Lamenting the indifference of your children? There is a saying that 'You can't change the past but you can change the future'. It is your choice.

The basic principles of making choices are:

1. The best choices are ones which are made consciously and carefully. Be conscious about the choice you are making by expressing it out loud to yourself and by being very specific (e.g. "I choose to be fitter" lacks oomph; "I choose to walk half a mile every day for the next 4 weeks" is tighter and sets a clear goal). Be careful of the consequences of that choice - What will be the short term consequences? What will be the long term ones? Will there be consequences you cannot at the moment foresee? What might get in your way?

2. Saying 'yes' to one thing means saying 'no' to everything else. At its simplest, by saying yes to a walk in the country, you are saying no in that moment to going to the cinema, sitting at home, gardening, writing a letter to your MP, etc. More seriously, saying yes to marriage means saying no to other suitors or lovers –

although there are those who want their jam roly-poly *and* custard (with cream on top). A choice, saying 'yes', involves sacrificing one or more things in preference for another which has greater value or benefits. Some choices are mutually exclusive. By choosing to walk to the shops, you are saying 'no' to going by car, it just is not possible to do both. Other choices are less black and white. You can choose to eat everything on the menu (although this could be unwise) or you can consciously and carefully choose the dish you most strongly prefer; having, say, fish and chips while sacrificing the lamb shanks or sirloin steak.

Choosing between alternatives is a skill and it is one which can be learned.

Making Choices

Begin by becoming aware that even your simple everyday actions are a choice; you either do it or you don't. As a warm-up before undertaking more strenuous exercise, start by making simple choices which have no far-reaching consequences. You do this by bringing into conscious awareness the fact that a choice is being made and by silently saying to yourself:

"I consciously choose to......" :

- turn off the alarm clock

- go into the bathroom

- pick up my toothbrush

- put toothpaste on the brush

- turn on the cold tap

- brush my teeth

-etc.

When you have mastered bringing these simple choices

into your awareness, move on to the next step of consciously choosing between alternatives. At this stage keep it light and fun, making sure that you are not making choices between things which have heavy consequences attached to them (such as adopting a Yak or getting married). Again, be aware that a choice is being made and silently say to yourself:

"I consciously choose to ..... rather than ....."

- brush my teeth with my left hand, rather than my right

- drink tea, rather than coffee

- eat an apple, rather than a flapjack

- walk on the sunny side of the street, rather than the shady side

- have fish and chips, rather than lamb shanks

-etc.

By this point you will be increasingly skilful in and aware of making choices.

Now is the time to make conscious choices between alternatives of increasing importance where you are choosing something which has greater value for you than the other possibilities. This is a form of trade-off and now that you have mastered trading-off simple things such as menu choices, you can up the ante and make choices between items of greater importance, achieving a balance of 'costs' and 'benefits'.

Be consciously careful in the choices you make by being aware that what you are choosing offers benefits which are greater than those of the alternative(s) you are sacrificing.

As before, say silently to yourself:

"I consciously choose to ..... in preference to ....."

> - book tickets for a week at the Edinburgh Festival in August in preference to renting a villa in Tuscany

> - buy a new washing machine in preference to a new greenhouse

> - travel to see my daughter in Devon in preference to having afternoon tea with Dolly at The Savoy

> - etc.

In each case weigh the benefits so that you are absolutely certain that a week in Edinburgh is of greater value to you than time in Tuscany; that the new washing machine is of greater import than the greenhouse; that Dolly comes second to your daughter on this occasion.

Having read this, you might be feeling the dead hand of the accountant pressing down on your decision making. Indeed, how dull life would be if all choices involved such deliberation and there were no room for spontaneity.

This exercise is training, a step on the road to mastery, and while it may seem simple, it is more stretching than it might at first appear. How uninteresting would learning the piano be if all you ever did was play scales? Like the one octave C major scale, it is practice. It is not in itself a work of art – more a step in the development of your technique and it may be a bit of a slog initially. Later, as you become more practised, it will be so much second nature that you will think of it in the same way as Lang Lang might regard a one octave scale when he is playing the *Hammerklavier* Sonata (Beethoven's most challenging work for the piano). Nor does it preclude fun or spontaneity - you can still make exciting, impulsive choices (although I counsel caution if Yaks or wedding bells are involved) and the fact that you are doing this with awareness need not detract from the pleasure.

You can turbo-charge your ability to make choices by making them with the super-powered ingredient of Will. The Will (with a capital W) is not to be confused with willpower which is harsh, stern and forbidding. The purpose of the Will is to direct, not to force. "Once, when the conductor, Herbert von Karajan was coaching his students, he made the distinction between laborious doing (willpower) and effortless direction in a marvellously clear fashion. He recalled the days when, as a child, he took riding lessons. On the night before his first jump he was sleepless with worry: 'How can I lift this enormous thing up into the air and over the fence? I thought to myself. Then I realised that no one lifts the horse. You set it in the right position and it lifts by itself. The orchestra will do the same thing.' "[25]

When you have no Will or 'effortless direction', the gap is filled with negative energies - anxiety, confusion, despair, bewilderment, uncertainty. The Will is important when making choices. Begin by reviewing the current state of your own Will:

Your Will

Think about the major relationships in your life - partners, family, friends – then ask yourself the following questions and write your answers in your Journal.

Do you:

1. Allow yourself to be pushed around by other people?

2. Give in easily to others' demands?

3. Give up rather than push on?

4. Get easily distracted from the task at hand?

5. Become paralysed with doubts and uncertainty?

6. Do what you truly want to do because you have willed it?

---

[25] Quoted in *Ferrucci, P. What we may be.* Turnstone Press, 1989, p77

If your answer to questions 1 to 5 is 'Yes', there is an opportunity for you to move from a state of having limited Will (or no Will at all). You can develop your Will and hence strengthen your ability to make choices with effortless direction by going through the following:

Developing Your Will

You can develop your Will by using it. Below are some suggestions for ways in which you can do this.

They do not require heroic acts of courage or that you put yourself in danger. These steps are safe, simple but effective.

Actions	Examples
1. Do something new.	*If you only read newspapers on Sunday, read a novel instead, or vice versa.*
2. Do something you do regularly but in a different way (e.g. or for longer, or, more slowly / faster than usual).	*Wash up very slowly, paying attention to every action.*
3. Make a plan and stick to it.	*Make a list of actions you want to take to de-clutter a room, and then do it.*
4. Do something which is the opposite of what others expect.	*If you always have a cappuccino and a caramel slice when meeting friends at a tearoom, have tea and carrot cake instead.*
5. Do something NOW	*Go and weed the garden*

rather than delay.	*NOW rather than waiting until the weekend.*
6. Delay doing something you would rather do now.	*Put off having a coffee and biscuit for an hour.*
7. Break a habit.	*Try going to bed half an hour later or earlier.*
8. Do something which is just outside your comfort zone.	*Invite some people for a meal who you don't know very well.*

Now that you are fully equipped to bring choice into your life and to do so using your Will, remind yourself of where we started: "Life is a choice. It is YOUR life. Choose consciously, choose wisely, choose honestly." You can choose, you always have a choice.

4
Letting Go

Having read and digested the fact that you have the freedom 'to choose your own way' and 'to choose any or several attitudes and activities', you will know that you are at liberty to choose whether to hang on to an idea which causes you pain or to let it go. There are two important concepts in that last sentence which warrant more explanation:

1. It is part of the human condition that you become attached to ideas about who you are, how other people should think and behave, and how the world should be. It is your attachment to these ideas which gives rise to your suffering. These ideas are nothing more than ideas and it is an illusion (or delusion) to see them as being reality however real they might seem.

2. Letting go of these ideas is not done easily and it may seem that hanging on is preferable to letting go; the ideas that you have built up over the years, the maps in your head that you have created painstakingly and coloured-in diligently, are familiar and, perversely, can be comfortable, even, enjoyable! It is difficult to confront or let go of whatever it is that is keeping you stuck and the difficulty comes from a fear that if you let go of what you've got, there will be nothing there but emptiness.

Letting go releases what has kept you stuck and allows space for the new to emerge. It also radically reduces your suffering. You will remember that 'at the root of suffering is attachment'; if the root is uprooted it follows that being no longer attached, suffering will wither and, eventually, cease. Suffering is denied its life force, there is non-attachment and, as any passing Buddhist will tell you, this is a concept which is central to their philosophy.

43

First, an anecdote about passing Buddhists. Several years ago I was standing at a bus stop in Croydon. Coming down the street towards me were a man and a woman whose beauty astounded me; they had about them an aura of calm and a glow of serenity. They were more vibrant and alive than anyone I had seen in a long while. As they passed behind me, I turned to look at them but they had completely disappeared. Curious, I moved to see where they had gone. It was then I noticed a sign which said "Croydon Buddhist Centre". Ah!

Buddhism focuses on craving (attachment) and how that craving brings sorrow. *The Dhammapada*, the words of the Buddha, teaches that all suffering stems from desire and that the way to attain freedom is to purify the heart and follow the way of truth.

> *"But whoever in this world overcomes his selfish cravings, his sorrows fall away from him, like drops of water from a lotus flower."*

> *"If the roots of craving are not wholly uprooted, sorrows will come again and again"* [26]

Non-attachment is about letting go of people, objects or ideas to which we adhere. The suffering comes from our clinging – from an unhealthy or exaggerated hanging on. Joanna is a snob. As a young adult, she would be disparaging about other people whom she regarded as being inferior to herself. Her young friends found this amusing and none of them took it seriously. It was simply Jo being witty and waspish, although some who met her thought she was cruel and lacking compassion. What Jo said was only one tenth of what she was thinking, so comments such as "My dear, what does she think she looks like? A pregnant cow?" were only the tip of the iceberg. Over time this judgmental thinking put down deep roots and her friends, wondering and worrying about what Jo might be saying about them, melted away to the point where she found

---

[26] The Dhammapada, Chapter 24, verses 336 and 338

herself alone and isolated. Her attachment to being superior to other people is at the root of her suffering.

Steve's suffering arises from his unwillingness to let go of being a victim. As a child he was bullied by his father, at school he was ridiculed for his tallness and clumsiness, in all of the many jobs he had, he found himself working for domineering, bullying men. In retirement, he volunteered as a helper at a local charity shop where he was abused by the full-time manager. He is attached to being a victim.

Both Joanna and Steve are creating their own suffering. They are attached to an idea which is not the reality. By letting go of their attachments, they would experience freedom and lightness, but they, like many people, are unwilling to let go. At a level which is most likely unconscious, Jo fears that her own shortcomings will be exposed if she does not get in with the first strike; Steve will have to face up to taking control and responsibility for his own life.

As the old ideas will die, they will not leave an empty hole, since new ones will appear. The loss of a significant relationship is a common experience – the lost love, the unrequited love, the ex-spouse or the deceased spouse – and the temptation is to hang on to the memory of the relationship for fear that there will be no-one to replace the vanished love. Until the fantasy (and that is what it is, a fantasy) is allowed to die and to take its rightful place in the chronology of a life, then it will have energy and power. Once it has been let go with appropriate grief, there will be a freedom which will create the space for new relationships and new possibilities to emerge.

Before I move on to the life cycle of the butterfly, a little more about grief. In the western world, grieving has a bad name, and nowhere more than in the UK, where, with our tradition of the stiff upper lip, and repression of feeling, any display of strong emotion is discouraged. This is not so in tribal communities, where members of the tribe lead communal keening to encourage and support those who are grieving in a full expression of their distress. The pain of the loss has to be experienced before it is possible to move on. Grief is not to be rushed, it is to be endured. If it is hurried, it will go underground and re-emerge; if it is pushed away, it will bounce back with renewed vigour; if it is covered over with sticking plaster, the wound will still be there. Back to the butterfly and letting go.

The closest physical analogy to letting go is that of the lifecycle of the butterfly. The caterpillar emerges from the egg and, as it grows, it sheds its skin four or more times so as to accommodate its rapidly growing body. The chrysalis is the transformation stage during which the butterfly's structure is formed. In the final stage, the butterfly emerges in its colourful splendour, fully mobile, ready to engage in courtship, mating, and egg-laying. As it grows, it leaves behind what it no longer needs in its development – the egg, the caterpillar and the chrysalis – but carrying forward those parts which are essential to its life. At each stage it has let go of something which is redundant so that something more splendid can emerge and grow.

Non-attachment

Non-attachment is not the same as detachment; nor is it the same as indifference. With non-attachment there is no longer a connection with the person or object or idea to which you were once attached. The thought or the memory does not have the power to gnaw or nag, to drag you down into unhappiness.

Detachment is not non-attachment because it contains aspects of denial and of self-defence. By detaching, you could be denying the thoughts which cause you pain, telling yourself that you don't really believe them, but this is an illusion. You are still attached, but not acknowledging that attachment; you think you are letting go, whereas you are cutting off. Detachment is a defence against pain or discomfort – if you say something is no longer important to you or doesn't matter anymore, you may be separating from 'it' but you are still attached. One way of detaching is to erect a protective shell around yourself to keep

46

the source of your distress at bay, but this does not mean that it loses its power.

Brian, recently 'given' early retirement from a managerial role with his local council, has begun to assert to friends and family that not only is retirement the best thing that ever happened to him, but that he never really enjoyed the work anyway. In spite of this, he often talks to his wife, Robyn, about his former colleagues and speculates about 'what's going on at the office'. Robyn knows how much he is missing being at work and how he feels he has been thrown on the scrapheap. She has noticed that, when she mentions his working life or his feelings about retirement, he cuts her off abruptly and is prickly and defensive. Brian, however hard he works at suggesting that he is detached from the past, is still in its grip.

Indifference is not non-attachment because it does not make the pain go away. However much you may protest that the losses you are experiencing or the fears you have of getting older are unimportant or don't matter, they are still there and have the ability to cause you suffering. Mel, who has been divorced from Ed for three years, is quick to say she doesn't care about him and that he can do what he wants. "It's his life, I don't care," she retorted when told he had a new girlfriend, but her friends know that she does care and this news pains her. In spite of her insouciance, she is still attached.

Whether you opt for detachment or indifference, the source of your pain is still alive and kicking. Once you feel you cannot tolerate the pain and suffering caused by your attachment, then is the time you will begin to make moves to let it go. When you are non-attached to the upsetting stuff going on in your head (which is where non-physical pain resides), you will enjoy freedom from suffering and experience true contentment. The more you can practise non-attachment, and the more you are able to be non-attached, the easier it will become and the happier you will be.

How to do this? It takes commitment and requires work. This is not to say it should not be attempted, for the reward is worth the effort.

You can develop non-attachment through meditation. Meditation means different things to different folks. One definition is: "Meditation is a practice of concentrated focus upon a sound, object, visualization, the breath, movement, or attention itself in order to increase awareness of the present moment, reduce stress, promote relaxation, and enhance personal and spiritual growth."[27] I see meditation as a process which will heighten your awareness so that you have more freedom to choose what your responses are going to be to any given situation so that, for example, when you find yourself in circumstances that would normally make you anxious, you can choose instead to be patient and calm. Meditation will help you develop the ability to pay close attention to your experience which will give you insights into how to become happier and more fulfilled.

When you read the word 'Meditation', in the last paragraph, what did you think? If you meditate regularly you will know the benefits it brings – physical, mental, emotional and spiritual, and the feeling of inner peace. If you have never meditated, you may imagine that you have to sit cross-legged on the floor and empty your mind for hours at a stretch. Don't be too alarmed. I am going to teach you a simple form of meditation which does not have to involve the lotus position and it is better that you meditate for a short time you enjoy than for a longer period when you can become uncomfortable and restless. It is called the 'Mindfulness Of Breathing' and is the foundation of all meditation practice and an excellent place to begin. It is simple and direct – all you have to do is be aware of your breath. You will find it described in the section on Developing Mindfulness in Chapter 13.

---

[27] Definition from http://medical-dictionary.thefreedictionary.com/meditation

Letting Go of Old Beliefs and Outmoded Ways of Thinking

The pace of change in the world has been very fast. Anyone who had been cryogenically frozen fifty years ago and reheated today would be alarmed by the revolution in standards of dress and manners, by the new technology (just think of personal computers, laptops, mobile phones, digital TV and TV sets), the ubiquitous supermarkets, the motorway network, the rise of India and China as economic powers, etc. You don't have to have had your body deep-chilled for 50 years to feel as if you have been dropped onto a different planet; your mind can be iced-up in the past too.

Beliefs, inherited from parents, teachers and other authority figures, are the rules you live by. They influence your values, your thinking, your emotions and your behaviour. Consider attitudes to homosexuality. Even after the Sexual Offences Act 1967, which legalised homosexuality, it was not until the 1980s that attitudes began to soften to accommodate the change. Today, when civil partnerships are recognised, there is a tolerance towards gay people that would have been unthinkable thirty years ago. That is not to say that everyone is tolerant and for older people brought up in more rigid and straitlaced times, this change can be difficult to accept.

Nicola has invited her grandson to stay for the weekend. He calls her to say he'd love to come and casually mentions that he will be bringing his boyfriend with him and is that OK? Rory is in his mid-thirties and has been with his partner for 10 years, nevertheless Nicola is vexed about what her neighbours will think and whether she should put them in separate rooms or together. The more she thinks about it, the more wound up and confused she becomes. She calls her daughter who tells her it is none of her business who Rory sleeps with and concludes by saying "Get with it, mother, who cares?"

After several sleepless nights Nicola rings Rory and tells him that something urgent has come up and she will have to cancel. No-one is convinced and bitter tastes are left in several mouths. Depressed by all this, Nicola decides it is time to 'get with it' and ditch her inconvenient beliefs about homosexuality being wrong and disgusting..... but how?

Letting go is not solely about jettisoning inconvenient beliefs. You may want to let go of an old way of thinking or feeling. For some older people, fears about ageing and illness can be paralysing; it is as if they are numbed by fear of the future and, in the expectation of a grizzly old age, have stopped living. To truly live, you have to let go of your fears.

The exercise below will lead you through a visualisation which will enable you to let go of old, redundant beliefs, thoughts, feelings or fears.

Dumping The Old

Before doing this exercise you should relax your body.

Find somewhere to sit where you will be warm, comfortable and undisturbed. Wrap yourself in a light blanket to keep yourself warm. Let any sounds inside or outside the room float by like clouds in the sky.

Make sure both your feet are flat on the floor and your hands sit loosely in your lap.

First breathe out to empty your lungs and then breathe in to the slow count of 4, hold for the count of 2 and breathe out for the count of 6, pause for the count of 2 and then repeat 5 times.

Now breathe normally, noticing your stomach rise as you breathe in and fall as you breathe out. Allow your body to sink into the chair and feel yourself becoming heavy.

Find a single word which describes an old belief or thought or feeling or fear you wish to shed. Be objective. If the first word you choose evokes a strong reaction, search for another which has less pull.

Allow an image to emerge for the old belief / thought /

feeling / fear - it may be an animal, a plant or some other symbol; it may be bright and shiny, or dull and dirty – whatever it is, do not push it away. Gently allow it to take shape in your consciousness.

Imagine that you are binding this image of your old belief / thought / feeling / fear in thick sticky tape so that it is immobilised and cannot escape.

See yourself putting the image of your old belief / thought / feeling / fear into a very strong steel chest and then covering the chest in thick concrete so that what is inside can never get out.

Now see the concrete covered chest being transported out to sea on a boat and, when you have reached the deepest part of the ocean, see yourself pushing the chest in its concrete casing over the side of the boat and notice that because it is so very heavy it sinks quickly to the uttermost depths of the sea for all eternity.

Notice how the waves come together again and cover over where the chest sank. Take a moment to notice the difference in how you feel. Be aware of the enormous weight that you have shed and be thankful.

Return to the shore and the safety of dry land. Imagine yourself coming home, opening your front door and going into your house knowing that the old belief / thought / feeling / fear is gone forever and can never return. Be grateful and say out loud to yourself in a voice resonant with conviction: "I am free, (pause) I am free, (pause) I am free." And so you are and will ever be.

Letting Go Of the Past & Living In The Present

I will begin with two quotes:

> *"The secret of health for both mind and body is not to mourn for the past, worry about the future, or anticipate*

troubles, but to live in the present moment wisely and earnestly." [28]

"Life is available only in the present moment. If you abandon the present moment, you cannot live the moments of your daily life deeply." [29]

The message is to let go of the past and live life as it is right now, not as it was 20 or 30 years ago, but today, this moment. It is easy to forget the present and to slip back into past memories (which are always sunlit and happy, of course) or to project into the future (which is where worry lives).

As a first step, write a letter to yourself in which you forgive yourself for all the things you have done or failed to do. You can either do this for real – write it, stick it in an envelope and post it to yourself – or you can write this letter in your Journal. This will help you to clear any toxicity which may be hanging around from your past.

Aim to use language which is non-judgmental. Rather than writing 'I was a terrible mother', describe factually the ways in which you think you were a terrible mother 'I did not provide you with regular meals', 'I did not congratulate you when you passed your exams', 'I did not buy you new clothes'. Forgiveness sets you free, so whatever it is you need to forgive yourself for, write it down.

A Letter Of Forgiveness To Yourself

Here are some prompts to stimulate your thinking about forgiving yourself.

You may want to forgive yourself for:

- your thoughts

---

[28] The Buddha. Source unknown.
[29] Thich Nhat Hanh. Source unknown.

- your feelings
- your behaviour towards others
- self-destructive behaviour
- your childhood
- your adolescence
- your adulthood
- your family members
- your intimate relationships (as a lover, husband / wife / partner, mother /father, uncle / aunt etc.)
- your working relationships.

Find yourself somewhere to sit with a table where you can write.

Sit quietly, take a deep breath and allow yourself to settle into your chair as you breathe out slowly.

Begin to write without censoring the words that appear on the page.

Once you have written down the things for which you want forgiveness, look back at the list and write down 'I forgive myself for ...'

A couple of examples will help:

I did not provide my family with regular meals	I forgive myself for not providing my family with regular meals
I despised my mother	I forgive myself for despising my mother

You now have the choice of either posting the letter to yourself or closing your Journal and doing something different.

When you receive the letter or you return to your

Journal, you have another choice. Either you can:

- Reread what you have written. If you make this choice, I recommend that you read out loud the sections beginning 'I forgive myself for...'

- Or you can destroy the letter or cut the page from your Journal. This is an option because you have already written the words of forgiveness to yourself and rereading all your past transgressions may reactivate them.

The work is done. Set the seal on it by saying to yourself the following affirmation:

"I, (your name), forgive myself completely, love myself fully and release myself from my past."

Repeat this frequently.

Back to the present! The only moment you have which is real and concrete is the present moment. The past has gone, and the future has not yet arrived.

How to live in the present

Here are some ways in which you can practise living in the here and now.

1. **Appreciate and be grateful for every moment:** Be appreciative and grateful for everything as it happens. Consciously enjoy the cup of tea you are drinking - noticing its taste, its flavour, its colour, its texture - and be grateful that you have this drink. Because they present you with an opportunity for growth, be appreciative and grateful for the mishaps of the day, taking the learning and insights from whatever it is that happens to you and be thankful.

2. **Be aware of what you are doing:** Bring conscious awareness to what you are doing right now. I am typing as I write this and, at this very moment, I am noticing

54

the feel of the keys beneath my fingers and of the specific keys I am touching to produce the letter(s) I need. When you are washing up, be fully aware of washing up, of the feel and temperature of the water, the suds, the dish you are cleaning right now.

3. **Love whatever you are doing:** At the Findhorn Community[30] in NE Scotland, they describe work as "love in action". This helps to make boring, routine tasks more tolerable. If you are cooking, do your cooking with love; if you are cleaning windows or the loo, clean with love. There is a story of three stonemasons who were asked what they were doing - one replied that he was earning a living, another that he was cutting stone, and the third that he was building a cathedral. What are you doing? Are you doing it grudgingly or with love?

4. **De-clutter and Spring clean:** Possessions are a way of hanging on to the past. Why are gurus and wise men usually people who have threadbare clothing and beg for food wherever they go? They are practising living in the present, seeking only to provide for their immediate needs. Are you surrounded by photographs of people and places from the past, souvenirs from past holidays? You cannot be living in the now surrounded by the memories of the past.

5. **Forgive:** Hanging on to old resentments or hatreds is damaging to your present day health. Resentment is like hammering a nail into your hand and hoping someone else will feel the pain. You cannot be free if you are tied to something in the past, so forgive and move on. Bring to mind the person or event you resent or regret, see them clearly in your mind and say out loud "I forgive you and bless you. May you be well, may you be happy, may you be free from suffering".

6. **Think and talk about the present:** Resting on your

---

[30] The Findhorn Foundation is a spiritual community in northeast Scotland, close to the village of Findhorn, near Inverness.

past (and wilting) laurels is boring to others - "When I was Captain of the golf club...." is probably only of interest to you and limits what you are doing today now that your captaincy is 25 years behind you.

7. **Tomorrow has not yet arrived:** If you are busy worrying about what might happen tomorrow, you will not be living today. Tomorrow will happen whether you worry about it or not, so why ruin today? Distinguish between worrying about tomorrow and planning for tomorrow - if you have to be at the station to catch the 07.30 then put your energy into planning rather than worrying.

8. **What worked yesterday, may not work today:** The answer to yesterday's problem ("If X happens, do Y") may not work today because the world has moved on. Be flexible in your thinking and behaviour, giving yourself a range of choices - "If X happens, then I could try Y or Z or A or Q" – so that you are free to choose whichever is most appropriate today.

9. **Do acts of random kindness:** I once gave a homeless young man in a subway at Hyde Park the sandwich which I had just bought from a shop; he was overwhelmed with gratitude and I felt good too. I had shifted my focus from myself and my needs to someone else and his needs. Do something spontaneously which involves you helping or giving up something for another person –a young mother carrying her pushchair up the steps, your seat to someone who is infirm, some money to the next charity that sends you a request for donations. You will feel one heck of a better person! And, by the way, distinguish between (a) feeling good about yourself because you have done an act of kindness (b) expecting something in return, and (c) pride.

10. **Be active:** sitting in a chair scanning the newspaper for evidence of all the ills in the world, watching TV, surfing the net, are passive and keep you stuck. Get up and do something active or creative – write a letter to a friend,

do some gardening or cleaning or knitting, ring your sister, go for a walk, do some stretches.

To conclude, it is important to your psychological and mental wellbeing (and hence to your physical health) that you live as much as is possible in the present moment. Being realistic – see chapter 8 – the challenge of living 100 per cent in the present is one which is achieved by only a very few; nevertheless, it is a worthy undertaking. As with any new venture, you will find it easier to take small steps initially, aiming to be completely in the 'now' for a few minutes and then gradually increasing this time.

5.
Acceptance

When faced with uncomfortable or painful situations you have three choices:

> 1. To fight and resist and in so doing aggravate the problem and give it energy.
> 2. To give up in despair. This does not make the problem go away and serves only to make you feel powerless and helpless.
> 3. To accept things just as they are. This will starve the crisis of energy and deny it its power.

The concept of starving ideas, thoughts, feelings and people of energy is demonstrated by this story:

> An older Cherokee man is teaching his grandson about life.
> "A fight is going on inside me," he says to the boy. "It is a terrible fight and it is between two wolves. One is evil. He is anger, envy, sorrow, regret, greed, selfishness, arrogance, self pity, guilt, resentment, inferiority, lies, false pride, superiority and ego. The other is good. He is love, joy, peace, hope, serenity, humility, kindness, benevolence, empathy, generosity, truth, compassion and faith. This same fight is going on inside you and inside every other person."
> The grandson thinks about it for a minute and then asks his grandfather, "Which wolf will win?"
> The old man replies, "The one you feed." [31]

Acceptance is not resignation, nor is it giving-in or giving-up. It is neither submissive nor passive. It is transformational, especially when things have happened that cannot be changed. On November 27th 2000, Damilola Taylor, a

---

[31] Author unknown. Source: http://www.sapphyr.net/natam/two-wolves.htm

10 year old boy was murdered in the stairwell of a block of flats in Peckham, southeast London. The death of a child has to be top of the list of the very worst things that can happen to a parent. One year later, his father, Richard Taylor, was able to say: *'When Damilola was killed on this day one year ago my life was devastated. It was destroyed...Gradually I felt that pain easing and I now realise that things happen in life for no reason, that's how God wants it to happen and there's nothing we can do about it. Damilola's was a short but good life. We thank God for him, he changed our lives and the memory of such a boy and his terrible loss will remain with us forever.'* [32]

None of us can know how Richard Taylor has come to accept the death of his son. Two things stand out from his words: that things happen for no reason, and that he thanks God for a short but good life. He could have blamed Damilola's killers, social workers, the police, society, the government, God, for taking his son from him with no reason, instead he chose to take the next step and thank God for Damilola's life and, in so doing, he was collaborating with the inevitable and accepting his terrible loss.

There is a trite saying "Pain is inevitable. Suffering is optional". Pain is a reality of life and it cannot be made pleasant or comfortable. Suffering is a choice – or, at least, there is a choice as to what degree of suffering you allow for yourself – and it can be a stepping stone to something greater. In Christian teaching suffering is something to be endured, the reward will come in Heaven. If this is so, then it suggests that you do what you can to cope with the suffering, stick a giant Band-Aid on it, and wait for the after-life. If it is not so, what then is the purpose of suffering? I believe it is an impulse towards wholeness; a push to grow; a pointer that something needs to change; a creative opportunity for transformation. One way to grow, if you choose, is to make friends with the source of the distress and bless the obstacle. This is what Richard Taylor did; he thanked God for Damilola who had changed their lives.

---

[32] The Times, November 28th 2001

Blessing The Obstacle [33]

Before doing this exercise you should relax your body.

Find somewhere to sit where you will be warm, comfortable and undisturbed. Wrap yourself in a light blanket to keep yourself warm. Let any sounds inside or outside the room float by like clouds in the sky.

Make sure both your feet are flat on the floor and your hands sit loosely in your lap.

First breathe out to empty your lungs and then breathe in to the slow count of 4, hold for the count of 2 and breathe out for the count of 6, pause for the count of 2 and then repeat 5 times.

Now breathe normally, noticing your stomach rise as you breathe in and fall as you breathe out. Allow your body to sink into the chair and feel yourself becoming heavy.

Remember a recent time when there was pain or suffering in your life. Go back to this moment and recall your emotions, your thoughts, your physical sensations, seeing what you saw, hearing what you heard and feeling what you felt. See this experience in your mind's eye as vividly as you can - turn up the volume on any sounds, brighten the colour on any images, bring the images closer. Let yourself experience the pain and distress you felt as fully as possible.

Now step out of this experience by standing up and moving to another chair or to a different part of the room. See all the component parts of your pain and suffering laid out before you. Say out loud: "I bless this (fear, pain, distress, or failure)."

Continue to look at this experience as if you are a detached observer of the fear, pain, distress, or failure.

---

[33] Adapted from Parfitt, W. *The Elements of Psychosynthesis*. Element Books, 1994.

Make the blessing statement out loud at least 5 times, allowing a pause between each statement, each time noticing how your memory of the experience changes. Allow it to become lighter and less attached to you. With the final statement, imagine it floating away up into the sky and far away.

Finally, be aware of what you have learned from the suffering. Be positive. Do not look for negatives. Once you have taken the learning, say out loud: "I choose to move on". Stand up and walk out of the room.

An Example of Blessing The Obstacle

Relax your body as described above.

Maggie was deeply upset when her daughter announced she would not, as was customary, be spending Christmas with her but was going to stay in London and spend the time with friends.

She was able to recall very clearly the rejection, the tears springing to her eyes, the sensation she had of being punched in her stomach, the feeling her bowel was going to empty, the impending loneliness, the embarrassment of telling her friends that she would be on her own over the holiday. She heard her daughter's words 'I won't be coming up at Christmas', she saw herself gripping the phone tightly, and re-experienced the anger and hurt she felt.

She turned up the volume of the words, brightened the picture of her sitting with the phone, and brought the image close so she could see her own face. What she felt most acutely was rejection.

Letting the image go, Maggie saw the parts that caused her the pain - the words, rejection, anger, hurt, loneliness. She imagined them lined up on the floor in front of her and, again, it was the rejection that stood out for her, so she focused her attention on that. She said "I bless the rejection". She paused, took several deep in-breaths, exhaling slowly before she again said "I bless the rejection". She repeated the sequence of breathing followed by the statement another 3 times.

She then moved to a different position in the room from where she could see the rejection from the point of view of an observer, watching herself watching the rejection. She repeated "I bless the rejection" 5 times, each time pausing to move to a slightly different perspective from which to observe. With each repetition, Maggie noticed the rejection lifting. Afterwards she said "It was as though it was shrivelling up before my own eyes". As she said "I bless the rejection" for the last time she imagined it floating up out of the room like a hot air balloon.

The learning for Maggie was that it was all right to feel upset, that she could get over it and she could handle being on her own. She would make plans to see friends, have people over for a meal, buy a couple of DVDs for the evenings or get some books. She also realised that her daughter had her own life, her own friends and she was pleased that she had had the courage to tell her that she would like to stay in London.

She finished by saying: "I choose to move on". When she stood up and walked out of the room she felt lighter, freer and optimistic.

Maggie has made the choice not to hang on to the pain of her daughter's rejection but to let go of the hurt (and of her hopes and expectations of a cosy Christmas) by blessing the rejection, choosing to accept it and to move on to make other plans. Her acceptance is liberating. She may, to be sure, return to it occasionally, but it will have lost its sting and its power.

6.
Gratitude

Being grateful, or cultivating gratitude, takes time and effort - it took Damilola Taylor's father a year to thank God for his son's short but good life - but it will be worth the outlay. To be grateful requires that you live in the present moment and consciously observe everything you are grateful for, however trivial.

To get you started, let's look at some of the things I have been grateful for today:

- Walking my dog in the fields near my home with the sun breaking through the morning mist;
- The birds singing cheerfully;
- My dog;
- My breakfast of poached eggs on toast;
- Knowing a close friend is coming up from London this weekend after time apart.

The things you choose (that word again!) to be grateful for do not have to be especially deep or philosophical. Start with the small things, however mundane they may be, and observe how these help you to enjoy life. By doing this you will begin to widen your field of observation. There is a lot in life we do not notice, so observation will open your eyes to what is already in your life and make you aware of previously obscured blessings. As you move around your home or garden or when you are out somewhere, become aware of what you are noticing and say to yourself: "I am grateful for ......"

Be grateful for what you have. Make a mental list of all the things you have in your life that you are grateful for, especially those you take for granted - your home, your furniture, your car, your pets, the people who help you, the friends you have, your family, your neighbours, your community, the food you eat, the fact that food is readily available, the plants in your garden that were gifts from friends, etc. You will be surprised at how long the list is once you get going, and you will also realise how well off you are compared to many others. Be grateful for your good fortune at having all these blessings in your life.

As your skill at being grateful increases – and within about 2 or 3 weeks it will – notice the acts of kindness of others. These do not have to be acts of martyrdom, or sacrificial offerings; just someone asking how you are, or showing interest in you and what you are doing, helping you by holding a door open for you, or inviting you into their home, are small but significant acts of thoughtfulness and humanity. Let them know that you are grateful and say 'Thank you'.

To begin to develop a sense of gratitude do the following:

Developing Gratitude

Think of a time in your life which has great meaning for you; this may be a moment when you felt to be on another plane - a moment of deep joy or bliss. For you this may be the day you got married, a time of intense intimacy with a lover, the birth of your child, standing on top of a high mountain, a moment in nature, listening to music - some kind of transcendent peak experience.

Close your eyes and return to this moment, remembering it in as much detail as you can, seeing what you saw, hearing what you heard, feeling what you felt. Make this memory as vivid as you can, as bright, as sharp and as colourful. Allow your body to be flooded with the sights, sounds and feelings of this wonderful time. Then consciously be grateful and say thank you, thank you, thank you.

What can get overlooked in the development of gratitude is appreciation of yourself! How much easier to beat yourself up than to build yourself up. Why not foster self appreciation? If you don't, no one else will..... and that sentence is not as flippant as it might seem. For other people to appreciate you, you need to appreciate yourself. Initially this idea might meet with some resistance because you might feel you would be guilty of pride, or because you would be embarrassed, or you wouldn't be able to think of anything or you're not worth it. Appreciating yourself is not being selfish and it will boost your self-esteem and confidence. Read through the list of qualities below and circle those that you feel apply to you:

Appreciating Yourself

able	delightful	invigorating	resilient
accepting	dependable	involved	resourceful
accountable	determined	joyful	respectful
accurate	devoted	joyous	responsible
achieving	diligent	just	responsive
adaptable	diplomatic	keen	robust
adventurous	direct	kind	romantic
affectionate	discerning	liberal	selfless
alert	disciplined	light hearted	self-aware
alive	discrete	likeable	self-confident
altruistic	discriminating	logical	self-disciplined
ambitious	dynamic	loving	self-reliant
analytical	easy going	loyal	sensitive
appreciative	eager	mature	serene
artistic	efficient	meek	sharp
assertive	empathic	merciful	simple
attentive	enduring	merry	sincere
aware	energetic	moderate	skilled
balanced	enlightened	modest	smart
benevolent	enterprising	moral	sociable
bountiful	enthusiastic	natural	soft
brave	exciting	non-	solid
bright	experienced	judgmental	special
broad-minded	expansive	nurturing	spiritual
calm	fair	obedient	spontaneous
candid	faithful	objective	stable
capable	far-sighted	observant	steadfast
carefree	fast	open-minded	strategic
careful	feeling	optimistic	strong
caring	fit	organised	strong-minded

cautious	flexible	orderly	strong-willed
centred	focused	original	successful
certain	forgiving	outgoing	supportive
charitable	free	passionate	sympathetic
charming	friendly	patient	systematic
cheeky	frugal	peaceful	tactful
cheerful	funny	peace loving	talented
child like	generous	perceptive	tenacious
civic minded	gentle	persevering	tender
clean	genuine	persistent	thankful
clear headed	good	personable	thoughtful
clever	good natured	persuasive	thorough
colourful	graceful	pious	thrifty
committed	grateful	playful	tolerant
communicative	happy	pleasant	tough
compassionate	harmonious	poetic	tranquil
compatible	helpful	polite	trusting
competent	honest	popular	trustworthy
competitive	hopeful	positive	unassuming
complete	humble	powerful	understanding
confident	humorous	practical	unique
congenial	idealistic	precise	unpretentious
conscientious	imaginative	profound	unselfish
considerate	independent	progressive	unwavering
consistent	industrious	punctual	uplifting
constructive	informal	purposeful	versatile
content	ingenious	questioning	vibrant
cooperative	innocent	quiet	vital
courageous	innovative	quick witted	warm
courteous	insightful	radical	wholesome
creative	inspirational	reactive	willing
cuddly	interested	realistic	wise
curious	interesting	reasonable	witty
decisive	intuitive	reflective	worthy
delicate	inventive	reliable	zealous

In your Journal you might want to transcribe those wonderful qualities that you circled in this exercise; this will make them more real and will heighten your appreciation of yourself. Spend time reflecting on these amazing qualities. What do they say about you as a person? Are there any qualities missing? If so, write them in your Journal as well. Are there any that you have not circled that you would like to develop? If so write these down and choose **one** that you would particularly like to work on using the exercise immediately below (you can revisit the others later).

You can use this exercise to develop any quality you wish and because this is a chapter about gratitude, the exercise below will help you to develop that quality by imagining yourself as already having it abundantly. By imagining it as fully as you are able, you will be bringing it closer to manifestation and to being a reality.

Developing The Quality Of Gratitude

Before doing this exercise you should relax your body.

Find somewhere to sit where you will be warm, comfortable and undisturbed. Wrap yourself in a light blanket to keep yourself warm. Let any sounds inside or outside the room float by like clouds in the sky.

Make sure both your feet are flat on the floor and your hands sit loosely in your lap.

First breathe out to empty your lungs and then breathe in to the slow count of 4, hold for the count of 2 and breathe out for the count of 6, pause for the count of 2 and then repeat 5 times.

Now breathe normally, noticing your stomach rise as you breathe in and fall as you breathe out. Allow your body to sink into the chair and feel yourself becoming heavy.

Bring to mind an image of yourself as already having the purest and most intense form of gratitude.

Allow the image of you to take shape and see the detail - notice the look in your eyes, your facial expression, your physical posture. Notice that you do indeed look grateful.

Hold this picture of you in your mind seeing the quality of gratitude intensify even further. Bring the image nearer, make it sharper, brighter and more colourful.

Imagine, and see, yourself walking into this image and

69

merging with it. Feel as if you are putting on a new set of clothes. Allow your body to be filled with this gratitude – it is flowing through your veins, inhabiting every cell. Gratitude is saturating your thoughts, your feelings, your attitudes.

Finally imagine yourself having gratitude in everyday situations where it would be of value to you. See gratitude expressing itself animatedly and in detail.

Using your Journal, you can further cultivate gratitude by spending five minutes each day writing down a list of the all the things from the day that you are thankful for, from the commonplace to the life changing. You will be creating a catalogue of the good things that have happened in your life and the act of recording them will engage your positivity and leave you with some happy memories you can read when things are not so bright.

A similar but different approach is to do an Evening Review:

Evening Review

Before you go to sleep at night nothing could be better or more restful than reviewing the agreeable things that have happened during your day. It certainly beats worrying about tomorrow!

Go through the events of your day and notice the ones you are grateful for. They can be momentous; invented anti-cancer drug, finished 9th Symphony, collected Nobel Prize, or they can be more run-of-the-mill. Went for a walk with Karen, had coffee with Ian, listened to an excellent play on the radio, bought a new washing up bowl, etc.

Keep it positive and be grateful. Conclude by saying Thank You.

You can boost your own sense of gratitude and well being by doing random acts of kindness for others. These random acts create a win/win situation: the person you are being kind to benefits from your help and the gratitude they feel makes you feel good for having helped them and reinforces a sense of gratitude within you. Never underestimate the impact of a single act of kindness.

20 Ideas For Random Acts of Kindness

1. Pick up litter you see in the street

2. Offer to babysit for young friends

3. Donate your used books to your local library

4. Offer to mow someone's lawn, walk their dog, clean their windows

5. Hold the door open for someone

6. Give a homeless person some food or cash

7. Mentor someone

8. Let someone go ahead of you in the queue

9. Buy a coffee for the person behind you at the coffee shop

10. Read to someone who cannot read

11. Thank your postman / woman or give him / her a gift

12. Write to, or phone someone who has made a difference in your life

13. Give a lottery ticket to someone

14. Personally thank someone who has served you

15. Treat a friend to a meal or the cinema

16. Tell a friend or family member how much you appreciate them and why

17. Let someone else have your parking space

18. Make a cake for a neighbour, or, take a meal to someone who is ill

19. Say hello to someone you see often but have never spoken to

20. Share your wisdom

Sharing your wisdom will stimulate your gratitude gland. You may not know it and may not feel it, but as you get older your store of wisdom increases; you have had a long life with many different experiences; you have learned from your mistakes, so why would you want to see others fall down the same deep hole in the same rutted road?

Be aware that willingness to receive your wisdom may vary by age and the nature of your relationship with the recipient. Young grandchildren and teenagers may well be more receptive to listening to their grandparents than your own children were at a similar age. There seems to be some built-in stubbornness between children and their parents which descends unbidden as they enter their teens, and this obduracy increases in direct proportion to the number and size of the axes to be ground. Mark Twain expressed this resistance pithily:

> "When I was a boy of fourteen, my father was so
> ignorant I could hardly stand to have the old man
> around.
> But when I got to be twenty-one, I was astonished at
> how much he had learned in seven years." [34]

Be selective in choosing with whom who you are going to share. Let the other person make the first move and look for signals that they are open to receiving. Young children and young adults have a way of expressing a need for advice which is

---

[34] Reputedly from: "Old Times on the Mississippi", Atlantic Monthly, 1874.

not always explicit or specific, so be attentive to the clues: "I don't know how / what / when / where to..."; "I can't do it", etc. Choose your moment. Be sensitive. Do not blunder in uninvited. The maxim "When the student is ready, the teacher (that's you) will appear" is apposite.

Gratitude takes time and effort. If you consciously develop an attitude of gratitude over 30 days, a new neural pathway[35] (which connects parts of the nervous system) will be established that will become stronger the more it is used.

---

[35] Neural pathways are built up when learning or having new experiences. For example, if you have a very painful experience like burning yourself, your brain will create a strong pathway to protect you from experiencing that pain again.

Amazing Ageing

The Six Pillars

Amazing Ageing

Be Positive

Be Realistic

Take Action

Be Flexible

No Rules

Be Resilient

7.

Be Positive

There was a time, not so long ago, when the attitude of the stereotypical Anglo-Saxon was to focus on the negative rather than the positive, on the downside rather than the up. Moaning was held in higher regard than merriment. Perhaps centuries of being slapped in the face with the wet flannel of disappointment (and the drizzle of a Temperate climate) had taught the nation to be wary of Mediterranean type happiness and this filtered down into the language – glasses are half full; chickens are not counted just in case, oops there goes another; fate is not tempted; we mustn't grumble, etc.

Now largely redundant, this archetype stands nevertheless as a reminder that life, and the way we handle it, is a choice. You can choose to be grumpy or happy. You can choose to think, feel and behave in whatever way you choose. People who are positive are more likely to:

- have more energy;
- be healthy;
- be more successful;
- and maybe to live longer.

Most positive people have chosen positivity as their default way of being. Remember Alice Herz-Sommer who, at 108, said that she had lived so long because she is an optimist: "I am an optimist, for me it's only the good things, never a bad thought"[36]. Why wouldn't you choose to be positive? What's not to like? Unless you are a pig-headed pessimist with dyed-in the-wool negativity thrown in, you would choose positivity over negativity every time and any day of the week. And the bonus is that you can teach yourself to become more positive, or let's take a big risk, you can train yourself to BE eternally

---

[36] http://www.bbc.co.uk/news/magazine-18613263

unconditionally positive, and I am going to teach you how to be more positive, right now!

There are, at least, four ways you can go about transforming yourself from a deadbeat, drag-the-world-down-with-you negativist into an upbeat everyone-wants-a-bit-of-you positivist. For the detail junkies, the first comes from Cognitive Behavioural Therapy (CBT)[37]; the second and third from Neuro Linguistic Programming (NLP); and the fourth from Psychosynthesis. So much for the long words and the fancy acronyms, what do they do? All the approaches involve changing your thinking without the help of men in white coats, brainwashing, or a lobotomy. The first focuses on challenging the way you talk to yourself by disputing the unhelpful, negative messages you are unconsciously giving yourself. It calls a halt to the negativity you are injecting into your brain minute by minute. The second also challenges the voice in your head by drawing attention to the poison you are pouring into your own ears and questioning the validity of this toxic rubbish. The third changes the way you look at events by reframing the content or by reframing them in a different context, and the final one invites you to meet the part of yourself that is self-critical.

1. A-B-C-D-E

A = Adversity. The event that precipitates a burst of negativity.

B = Beliefs. Which impact on how you interpret the adversity / event.

C = Consequences. The feelings or behaviour which result.

That's enough to start with. Before moving on let's look at an example:

> **A** Halfway through a meeting, your colleague suddenly leaves the room, slamming the door as he

---

[37] Taken from Learned Optimism by Martin Seligman.

leaves.

B You think: "It must have been something I said. He's obviously bored and irritated. Now he'll hate me and won't talk to me ever again."

C You feel angry, disappointed and tearful.

Terrific! What a great meeting you're having..... and how easily this can spin out of control into anxiety, misery and depression.

However, D and E ride to your rescue.

D = Distraction and Disputation. Distract yourself by doing something else or question the belief by searching for evidence to support or dispute it, looking for what alternative explanations there might be, exploring what the implications of holding that belief are and what value holding it has for you.

E = Energisation. What you felt, thought or did next.

A Halfway through a meeting, your colleague suddenly leaves the room, slamming the door as he leaves.

B You think: "It must have been something I said. He's obviously bored and irritated. Now he'll hate me and won't talk to me ever again."

C You feel angry, disappointed and tearful.

D You say to yourself: "It's nothing, I'll distract myself by looking out of the window until he comes back;"

Or: "I'll look at the facts - he always tells me how interesting I am and how he values my opinions. He's never done this before and there is no evidence he's bored"

Or: "Maybe his phone went off and he's gone to answer it and the wind caught the door so that it slammed"

Or: "If I'm right and he's bored or lost interest, I'll find ways of being more interesting"

Or: "It is destructive to think he'll never talk to me again. I'm not even going to go there!"

E You think: "I was able to relax and let go of the thoughts and feelings so that when he came back with a tray of coffee and biscuits, I was pleased to see him."

You get the idea? You look at the event, examine what belief lies behind your concern and how this makes you feel or behave. You then challenge this by either doing something else or by disputing it with the facts, by looking at other explanations or ways of handling it, and then as a result you feel more positive.

It is a common human reaction to respond to negative events by blaming yourself - "He left the room **+** slammed the door behind him **=** it's my fault". The incident described above can rapidly become a whirlwind of self-blame in you which get swept up into torrents of self-loathing. In being swift to take responsibility yourself, you may be overlooking the fact that there may be many, many other reasons why something happened. It is valuable to consciously put the brakes on your self-punishment, stand back and examine the facts, search for the evidence and dispute your distorted interpretation. In a moment you will have the chance to become aware that you are highly selective in the information you can process or allow in to your overcrowded brain. Being aware that you delete, distort and generalise enables you to be positive even when confronted by apparently negative events.

2. Deletion, Distortion & Generalisation

The amount of information you receive is so vast that you cannot process it all. Just think of the information you are subject to as you walk down a busy street: the goods in shop windows, the advertisements, the people, the sounds, the 'cross now / don't cross' signs. To cope with this you have developed the ability to be selective and to delete, distort or generalise the experience.

Deletion = You leave bits of information out. How many times have you passed someone you know in the street and they don't see you. Either they are deleting or being deliberately rude!

Distortion = More emphasis is given to some stimuli than others. If you are driving, changing traffic lights will be more prominent than a neon sign flashing in a shop window.

Generalisation = You generalise one example to be representative of the whole. This usually takes the form of "All xs are y". So you see one upmarket shop in the street and you generalise to "All shops in the High Street are upmarket."

While this skill is valuable in handling unmanageable amounts of data and stimuli, it is not helpful when applied to thought. Some examples are:

Deletion:

- "They won't like it"

Ask yourself specifically WHO won't like WHAT?

- "Golf is better for me"

Question yourself about in what way exactly golf is better for you? Better than what? Who says?

- "I'm useless"

Challenge yourself by asking specifically what you are useless at? Are you useless at everything all the time and everywhere? By whose standards?

Distortion:

- "They didn't invite us, I guess they don't like us"

Does the lack of an invitation mean that you are not liked? Perhaps there is another interpretation such as a limit on the numbers they could accommodate comfortably in their house, or you were invited last month and it is someone else's turn this month, or the invitation was not delivered, or it was a party for ex-colleagues or Koi carp aficionados?

- "The new milkman ignored me when I said hello"

Before you get upset, you might ask yourself whether perhaps he is hard of hearing, or whether English is his native tongue, or whether you spoke clearly enough.

Generalisation:

- "I should always wear a hat and gloves when I go shopping"

Hang on! Who says? Why should you? Just because your Granny wore hat and gloves to go to Barkers of Kensington, doesn't mean you have to wear them in Tesco.

- "It always rains when we go away".

What? Are you really saying that it has rained all the time on all the holidays you have ever taken? Has the sun never come out, ever?

- "I'm not assertive enough".

Do you never assert yourself or are there certain situations in which you find it more difficult? Who says that you're not assertive enough? What is enough anyway?

As with A-B-C-D-E you can benefit by becoming aware of the language you are using (or have someone point it out to you) and then by challenging it. Negative language and putting negative interpretations on language is draining and debilitating. Worse, negative ways of thinking such as "I'm useless", "Nobody loves me", "I'm lonely" can become habitual.

The last of these "I'm lonely" is one of the most corrosive thoughts to which ageing people are prey and, if you think this way, you could challenge your own thinking. Since it is a thought that most people would not be willing to share with others, you can confront it yourself by asking questions such as: Am I always lonely? Am I lonely all the time? Are there certain times when, or situations where, I feel more lonely? Am I alone or am I lonely? What could I do differently today? Who could I contact?

There is a difference between being lonely and being alone (see Chapter 14), and this is the subject of the next approach - Reframing.

3. Reframing

The concept of reframing is exactly similar to reframing a picture. You may have noticed that taking a painting or photo out of an old heavy frame and reframing it in a cleaner, lighter one changes your perception of the picture.

In the same way, this psychological reframing changes the meaning of an event or an experience by taking it out of its original (negative) frame and putting it into a different (positive) frame. This is usually a matter of simply changing the content of the language by word substitution. For example, you can change "I'm lonely" into "Right now I'm alone".

The former suggests that you are always lonely all of the time; the reframe allows the possibility that this is temporary, and the small change in wording takes the sting, the pathos and the tragedy out of the first statement and replaces it with something which is more palatable and has less, if any, stigma attached to it.

Another change of frame can be achieved by changing perspective, by looking at the same thing from another point of view.

Bill has had his car stolen and it has been written off. He says "What a disaster!"

Jim says "Great! Now you'll be able to get the Porsche you always wanted."

Wally says "You'll be able to get fitter by walking or cycling (until you buy your new Porsche)."

If you have persistent beliefs or opinions, you can change them from a negative frame to a positive frame:

Negative	Positive
"I'm useless"	"I may be useless at playing the oboe because I've never tried, but I am a botanical artist with two RHS Gold Medals"
"Nobody loves me"	"I don't have a regular lover, or even an irregular one. I do have a lot of friends, nephews and nieces who I know care very much for me"
"Halfway through the meeting he left the room slamming the door behind him"	"He needed coffee and was kind enough to bring me one too - and a biscuit!"
"I'm lonely"	"I am alone much of the time. I live on my own

	and work on my own. This means I can do whatever I want, whenever I want, and I don't have to answer to anybody. Ever!"
"I've got to go into a nursing home and I'm dreading it - all those ghastly old people!"	"If I'm not well, I'll get the attention I need when I need it- no more trying to get appointments at the surgery. And there'll be lots of people to talk to who will have their own interesting tales to tell. I'm excited"
"I'm nervous when I meet new people"	"When I meet new people I am excited"

The first step is to become aware of the words, phrases and thoughts that flit through your mind faster than you can say "I'm getting slow on my pins and my hearing is not what it was". Become consciously aware of what you are saying to yourself, of the messages you are repeatedly imprinting on your mind, consider how this has a damaging effect on your psychological wellbeing, and then change the language or look at it from another angle.

Think about some of the negative words or phrases you think or say about yourself, there will be plenty of candidates, and write a list of them in your Journal. If you put the negatives in the left column you will have room in the right column for the positive reframe. This is the first step; the second is to catch yourself using the negative phrase and then to replace it with the positive.

The last of the four ways in which you can transform your negativity is to meet up with the part of you that is self-critical. Self-criticism is an uncomfortable bedfellow of positivity; to increase your positivity it is very useful to integrate the self-critical part of yourself.

The technique below comes from Psychosynthesis, but first I need to describe the notion of subpersonalities. One of the central principles of Psychosynthesis regards a person as having not just one personality, but a set of different personalities or subpersonalities. I have many roles and play many parts - I am dog walker, businessman, cook, NLP coach, cleaner, gardener, therapist, driver, pianist, friend, lover – often all in the same day and I flit from one role to another with what I hope is seamless ease! These are the subpersonalities that I am aware of and can name, but there are others more hidden, less conscious and even repressed. It is as if there is a whole orchestra of different subpersonalities inside of me, and when these parts are synthesised and harmoniously integrated, I am like the conductor of an orchestra who can bring the different parts in to play at the appropriate time.

One of the most common subpersonalities which clients bring to the counselling room is the Inner Critic, that part of them which is self-critical. This is the part which can be both judgmental of others and fiercely critical of ourselves; it chips away at our best efforts, rebukes us for our 'faults' and destroys our self confidence and self esteem. It can present itself as charming but cunning, or as hard-nosed and ruthless.

Assagioli suggests that we give our subpersonalities humorous names both to lighten the exercise and to be aware that this subpersonality is not all of who we are. Let's go and meet your self-critical subpersonality.

4. Meeting Your Inner Critic

- Make yourself comfortable and ensure you are warm. Close your eyes.

- Begin by visualising your critical subpersonality. To do this, allow an image for your Inner Critic to emerge - it may be a symbol, an object, an animal or a type of person. If what emerges is a person you know or recognise, you have probably chanced upon a critical person rather than your critical subpersonality; if this is so, thank this person and move on until something less 'factual' and more unreal arises. This image is of consequence because it is a pathway into the unconscious, or, as Jung wrote, it "point(s) to something that is very little known or completely unknown." [38]

- Give your Inner Critic a humorous or friendly name.

- Visualise yourself going with this image of your subpersonality to a peaceful place such as a meadow. Create as full a picture of this place in your mind as you can. Together you and your subpersonality take in your surroundings: the grass and the flowers, the birds and the sounds of nature, the trees and a mountain.

- Go to the foot of the mountain with your subpersonality and begin the climb.

- Imagine the scenery you pass through as vividly as you can, seeing the rocks, the plants, the trees, the scrubby vegetation, the valleys below. Be aware that you are going higher and higher where the air is cleaner and the atmosphere is silent.

- Keep an eye on your subpersonality and notice any changes in its clothing, mood or appearance, as you make your ascent.

- As you get to the top, feel the sun shining down on both of you and stand directly in its light.

- Ask your subpersonality to communicate with you, prompting it with questions about what it needs. Listen

---

[38] Carl Gustav Jung. *Simboli della transformazione.* Torino, Broignhieri, 1970. p. 222.

to what it has to say without being judgmental or censoring anything.

• When you sense that the subpersonality is complete, thank it for coming and for being honest with you, return down the mountain together and back into the meadow.

• Gently open your eyes and come back into the room where you are sitting.

In your Journal record your recollection of this meeting with your self-critical subpersonality. What did it look like? What did it need? Are you able to provide what it needs, and if so, how? The visualisation above and your reflection and interpretation of it, is constructive work and it may be necessary to do it more than once – subpersonalities can be sly and devious. Your aim is to become fully acquainted with this part of you that you have probably pushed away for many years.

When you feel you are familiar with this self-critical part of you, you can "dis-identify" from it. This is not to disown it, but to put it in the context of your whole being; you move from being over-identified and driven by your self-critical subpersonality to being the dis-identified dispassionate observer. You are no longer controlled by it, but in control of it. Assagioli wrote: *"We are dominated by everything with which our self becomes identified. We can dominate and control everything from which we dis-identify ourselves ... Every time we "identify" ourselves with a weakness, a fault, a fear or any personal emotion or drive, we limit and paralyze ourselves. Every time we admit "I am discouraged" or "I am irritated," we become more and more dominated by depression or anger. We have accepted those limitations; we have ourselves put on our chains."*[39]

The Psychosynthesis Dis-identification Exercise can be used, not just to synthesise your subpersonalities within your overall personality, but whenever you are troubled or unhealthily

---

[39] Assagioli, Roberto. *Psychosynthesis.* Thorsons, 1995. P22

involved in a physical, mental or emotional state. You can dis-identify from whatever physical sensations, thoughts or feelings with which you have become over-identified, and you can find that strong, still, silent, observing centre of your self, which in the exercise is called the 'self' or 'I'.

Many years ago I recommended a friend of mine who was at the troubling end of a close relationship to use this exercise as many times a day as he could and, particularly, whenever he was flooded with emotion. He reported that with repeated use it was very calming.

Disidentification

• Find somewhere that you can be comfortable and undisturbed. Relax by breathing IN to the count of 4 and OUT slowly to the count of 6. Read the following silently or out loud or record it onto a tape / CD or an audio device:

• 'I am grateful for my body but I am more than my body. My body may find itself in different conditions of health or sickness, it may be rested or tired, but that has nothing to do with my self, my real I. I value my body as my precious instrument of experience and action in the world, but it is only an instrument. I treat it well, I seek to keep it in good health, but it is not myself. I have a body, but I am more than my body.'

• Close your eyes and reflect on what you have just read. There is no need to hurry, take your time. After a while, repeat 'I have a body but I am more than my body.'

• Now read the following silently or out loud: 'I am grateful for my feelings, but I am more than my feelings. My feelings and emotions are diversified, changing, and sometimes contradictory. They may swing from love to hatred, from calm to anger, from joy to sorrow, and yet my essence – my true nature – does not change. I remain. Though a wave of anger may temporarily submerge me, I know that in time it will pass; therefore I am not this anger. Since I can observe and understand my feelings, and can gradually learn to direct, utilize, and integrate them harmoniously, it is clear that they are not my self. I have feelings, but I am more than my feelings.'

• Close your eyes and reflect on what you have just read. After a pause repeat 'I have feelings, but I am more than my feelings.'

• Now read the following silently or out loud: 'I am grateful for my mind but I am more than my mind. My mind is a valuable tool of discovery and expression, but it is not the essence of my being. Its contents are constantly changing as it embraces new ideas, knowledge, and experience, and makes new connections. Sometimes my thoughts seem to be independent of me and if I try to control them they seem to refuse to obey me. Therefore my thoughts cannot be me, my self. My mind is an organ of knowledge in regard to both the outer and inner worlds, but it is not my self. I have a mind, but I am more than my mind.'

• Close your eyes and reflect on what you have just read. There is no hurry, so pause and then repeat 'I have a mind, but I am more than my mind.'

• Next comes the phase of identification. Affirm clearly and slowly to yourself silently or out loud: 'After this disidentification of my self, the 'I', from my body, my feelings, and my mind, I recognize and affirm that I am a centre of conscious awareness and Will.' Close your eyes and reflect on this. After giving yourself sufficient time for reflection, repeat 'I am a centre of conscious awareness and Will.'

• Once you have done this longer version several times, you can use the short form which is: 'I am grateful for my body and sensations, but I am more than my body and sensations. I am grateful for my feelings and emotions, but I am more than my feelings and emotions. I am grateful for my mind and thoughts, but I am more than my mind and thoughts. I am I, a centre of conscious awareness and Will'.

You have taken a significant stride forward in this chapter. Being positive is essential to your psychological and physical health. You have learned ways in which you can manage your negativity and transform it by:

- Disputing your negative feelings or the negative messages swirling around in your mind;

- Challenging the thoughts which have, through the process of deletion, distortion or generalisation, acquired a negative edge to them;

- Reframing the negative meaning you have attached to experiences, thoughts or feelings by putting in a different, positive frame;

- Having the courage to meet with your Inner Critic. By dis-identifying from this destructive sub-personality, you have simultaneously put yourself in a position of control and integrated this part of you with the rest of your personality.

8.
Be Realistic

Being realistic is to be real, interpreting your world as it really is with both your feet firmly on the ground, including both the positive and the negative, the good and the bad. In *The Velveteen Rabbit* by Margery Williams[40], two toys in a nursery discuss becoming Real:

> "Does it hurt?" asked the Rabbit.
> "Sometimes," said the Skin Horse, for he was always truthful. "When you are Real you don't mind being hurt."
> "Does it happen all at once, like being wound up," he asked, "or bit by bit?"
> "It doesn't happen all at once," said the Skin Horse. "You become. It takes a long time. That's why it doesn't happen often to people who break easily, or have sharp edges, or who have to be carefully kept. Generally, by the time you are Real, most of your hair has been loved off, and your eyes drop out and you get loose in the joints and very shabby. But these things don't matter at all, because once you are Real you can't be ugly, except to people who don't understand."
> "I suppose you are real?" said the Rabbit. And then he wished he had not said it, for he thought the Skin Horse might be sensitive. But the Skin Horse only smiled.

I urged you earlier to be positive because I believe life is easier and you will have a better outcome if you seek out the positive rather than search for the negative. 'Positive thinking' however is another matter; in my view it can coat your thinking in a saccharine glaze which, by ignoring the negative, distorts reality. You need to have both the positive and the negative to see the whole picture. Taking a realistic view of your world is important; if you choose to ignore lumps which appear in your body, or to walk alone at night in a dangerous neighbourhood, you are being naive and foolish.

---

[40] Williams, Margery. *The Velveteen Rabbit*. Running Press, US. !996.

It is one of the givens of ageing that it is more difficult to keep things in proportion. Concerns about lumps and aches in your body, about being mugged, about the state of your finances, your relationships with others, can spiral downwards into fear, anxiety, depression and hopelessness. Speculation, vagueness and fluffy thinking create fear. To dissolve your fear, stick to the facts, look for the evidence and make the issues as concrete and real as you can. Realists are people who look circumstances in the eyeball without flinching and take any necessary corrective action.

Peter has a weak bladder, for which he has sought medical attention, but, meanwhile, he needs, or feels the need, to urinate frequently. He is fearful that one day he will be unable to get to the loo in time and will wet himself, as a consequence of which he no longer goes to the theatre, cinema or concerts in case he feels the need 'to go'. Apart from the medical remedies which might help him and the practical steps he could take to minimise the risk (such as reducing his liquid intake in the hours beforehand and making sure he goes to the loo immediately before the event starts, etc), he should also stick to the facts and look at the evidence by asking himself how often in the past he has needed to get to the loo urgently, how often he has wet himself. If the answer to both questions is 'never', there is a very good chance that it will continue to be never; if it is 'once' there is a pretty good chance it won't happen this time; if it is 'frequently', that is a different matter and he needs to seek medical advice and change his behaviour accordingly.

Olivia used to be the sort of person who, the morning of going on holiday, would sling a heap of clothes into a suitcase, sit on the lid and make for the airport. How this has changed! A week or so before, she begins to worry about forgetting her passport, failing to book the cat into the cattery, cancelling the newspapers, making sure her mobile phone is charged, omitting to take a list of important phone numbers, remembering her insurance documents, tickets and so on. Once on the plane she worries about what she may not have done – did she turn the bedroom fire off, leave money out for the window cleaner, throw away the milk in the fridge? Olivia could reduce her pre-holiday anxiety by writing lists of what she has to do and crossing each item off the list as she deals with it. If her in-flight anxiety still persists, she could comfort herself by searching for the evidence that in the past she has come back from holiday to find her house burned to the ground, the windows dirty and sour milk in the fridge.

Given below are 10 ways in which you can practise being realistic:

Being Realistic

1. Be realistic about your **capabilities**. If you are compromised in any way, for example mobility or your ability to look after yourself, be realistic about what you can and cannot do. There is no reason why you should not flex your physical, mental and emotional muscles and try new things or try doing things in a different way, and if you find after several attempts that it is not working, then be realistic and either seek support or throw in the towel.

2. Be realistic about what you are **seeing, hearing and feeling**. You do not need to analyse everything or everyone's motivations, or create elaborate fantasies about what is going on. Take things at face value. If someone says they will have to cancel going to the cinema with you, take it as stated.

3. Be realistic in your **expectations** of yourself, of others, of life. Setting high expectations is setting yourself up for disappointment. If your partner has died and you have decided to plunge into the dating pool, it is unrealistic to expect to meet a carbon copy of your deceased who has the same qualities you admired and loved so much. If your expectations are grounded in reality, you will not be let down. Accept life for what it is.

4. Be realistic about **what you need** (rather than what you want). This is especially important if you are living on a tight budget. Become aware of what is necessary and what is

extra, and stick to the necessities.

5. Be realistic about **time**. You probably know children who 'want-it-and-want-it-now'. You are not a child. You can take as much time as you need. If you need more time than you used to, then take it. There is no need to hurry; rushing is stressful.

6. Be realistic in your **reactions**. React in proportion to the stimulus and pause to consider the appropriateness of your reaction. Anger is only an appropriate response to some situations.

7. Be **authentic** and be consistent. If you put on an act, you will be found out.

8. **Ask questions**. Making assumptions leads to making ill-informed decisions. Better to ask 'Is this a safe neighbourhood to walk at night?' than to assume it is.

9. Allow your **emotions** to show. There is a balance to be struck between schmaltzy and mawkish, and remaining cold and unresponsive. An appropriate display of emotion - excitement, anger, grief, joy - lets others know that you are real.

10. Be **accepting of failure**. Failure is only a form of feedback, sending you information that what you thought or said or did this time didn't work and you need to do it differently next time.

Keep your feet firmly on the ground, both literally and metaphorically. Heather has over the years acquired a reputation for being 'away with the fairies'; she is consistently unpunctual, forgets appointments, procrastinates, lives in a dimly lit, untidy house surrounded by mangy dogs, mounds of unwashed laundry and un-ironed ironing, and lurches from one financial drama to the next. Living in a twilight world where nothing is quite real to her, she bemoans her laborious life.

You, and Heather, can ground yourself by doing some simple activities:

Becoming Grounded

1. Ensure you are living your life from inside your body. If you feel you are floating somewhere off the ground, close your eyes and imagine that you have roots growing out of your feet and going down into the earth.

2. Spend time outside in nature. Be consciously aware of the ground under your feet. Look at the trees and see how they are held steady by strong roots going deep into the ground.

3. Do something physical. Walking is better for staying grounded than paragliding. Digging the garden gets you close to the soil. Chopping logs puts you in touch with a woody earthiness. Tending and nurturing plants connects with the rhythm of the seasons. Clean your house - you cannot be off the ground when you are on your knees polishing the kitchen floor.

4. Look after yourself and others. Time spent washing, cooking, ironing, exercising, tending to pets, being attentive to the needs of others, keeps you in touch with everyday life.

5. Be practical. Start those jobs which have been hanging around waiting for your attention. Do less thinking and concentrate instead on doing.

You have learned ways in which you can practice being realistic as well as some tips for keeping yourself grounded and in touch with reality. You can keep a sense of proportion by being clear what is important to you and what is not. Arthur Balfour, onetime Prime Minister, said "Nothing matters very much, and very few things matter at all".

9.
Take Action

Taking action is a powerful way to reduce anxiety and to stay grounded. Doing something is better than worrying about it Remember: "Today is that tomorrow you were worrying about so much yesterday." Taking action gives you confidence - once you have confronted something head on, sought for evidence and collected the facts, you have the confidence to do it again ... and again.

Heather, from the previous chapter, is unable to take action effectively. Hence the piles of washing and ironing, the untidiness, her unkempt dogs, and her inability to keep appointments or to arrive on time. Surrounded by this chaos, she feels powerless. In her book *Feel The Fear And Do It Anyway*, Susan Jeffers[41] suggests that our ability to act is determined by how we relate to fear. Her view is that fear affects people in one of two ways; either they are empowered by fear and respond to it from a position of power (choice, energy, action) or they are paralysed by fear (anger, helplessness, depression and inertia). Heather is not acting from a place of power and is avoiding taking charge of her life. As Jeffers says 'Action is very positive and very powerful'.

When you find taking action is difficult:

1. Silently say two affirming phrases to yourself - "Just do it" and "I can handle it";

2. Break the task down into smaller chunks. Going back to Olivia and the holiday example, it will be easier to complete all the tasks successfully and with a sense of achievement if the items on your list are in do-able chunks. Having one thing on the list – 'pack' – is the overall goal and something you will want to complete before you leave home, but it is too big a chunk to do in

---

[41] Jeffers, Susan. *Feel The Fear And Do It Anyway*. Vermilion. 2007

one go. If instead you break it down into: select clothes, wash clothes, iron clothes, pack beachwear, pack day-wear, pack evening-wear, pack toiletries, pack camera, pack maps and guidebooks, book Tiddles into cattery, cancel papers, leave money for window cleaner, empty fridge, check fire is off, etc, how much more satisfaction will you feel as you cross each item off the list!

How To Take Action

1. No Excuses - Do It Now!

Once you have decided to take action, do it now. Waiting only builds up the tension and anxiety which makes taking action more testing. OK, there may be obstacles and blocks in the way, but get started and keep going. Taking action is very empowering.

2. Be Powerful, Be Responsible

Blaming your circumstances or other people saps your energy; doing something about it puts the power and the responsibility back in your hands. When you realise that you are responsible for your own success (and your own failure), you will feel powerful.

3. Fear As A Friend

If you treat your fear as a friend, prodding you to do something and to take responsibility for it, then fear is no longer your enemy.

4. Focus on How - Not On What If

Putting your focus on how to do something, how to solve a problem, how to achieve a goal will clear your mind. Concentrating on what might go wrong will confuse it. While it is reasonable to anticipate and plan for some events, over-anticipation or excess anxiety can drain all the pleasure from an experience. When setting out on a 300 mile car journey, it is sensible to know that if you have a puncture, you will call the roadside assistance services, or, that if there is an accident on the motorway which delays you for several hours, you have a sandwich and a book and can listen to the radio; this is planning. What if I have a seizure? What if my brakes fail? What if a lorry comes round the corner on the wrong side of the road? These 'What ifs' are negative and neurotic. Focusing on the how puts your mind to good use and fosters a positive inner attitude.

5. Ask For Help

There is nothing shameful in asking others to help you. Whether it is learning to shop online or moving house, there will be people only too happy to help. Leave the feelings of embarrassment and shame behind. Asking for help is not a sign of weakness and does not mean you are a failure – think of the people who have asked you for help, were they losers? No! Did you gain from helping someone else? Yes! You cannot read other people's minds and they cannot read yours, so instead of thinking "I wish Quentin would ask me where I am going to stay on my way to visit", reframe your thinking to "I'll tell Quentin that I am going to be driving 300 miles and ask for his help to book an hotel room". Be clear and positive about what you want help with; while people are happy to help, they need to know exactly what is expected of them and they don't respond so well to whiners. And, of course, be grateful!

6. Small Steps

Action is easier if you take one step at a time. Small chunks are more digestible than big chunks and sometimes it is the first step, the small chunk, which starts the whole process of taking action. This may not be radical or exciting, or the grand gesture you were aiming for, but it is a start. A 300 mile car journey starts with you getting in your car!

7. Stay Present

Live in the present and be grateful for each small step you take, remembering that each one is bringing you closer to your goal. If you focus only on the ultimate goal, you are unlikely to feel any sense of achievement until you get there. It would be a rare person who was so focused on the end of the 300 mile journey that they took no pleasure in the changing scenery, the wayside stops, the meals and refreshments, the overnight stay in an hotel; a wise traveller would choose an interesting and varied route, a comfortable and friendly B&B for the night, and set small goals along the way with stops for coffee, lunch, a nap, a visit to a Museum or a National Trust property.

If, like Heather, there are aspects of your life of which you are not in charge, you can implement the steps above and reinforce this by visualising yourself taking control.

Taking Charge

• Make yourself comfortable and ensure you are warm. Close your eyes.

• Allow a symbol to emerge representing the part of your life which is out of control.

• Address three questions to the symbol and listen carefully for the answer. Resist the temptation to force anything and give the symbol time and space to provide you with the answer.

1. What do you want?

2. What do you really need?

3. What do you have to offer?

• Gently open your eyes and come back into the room where you are sitting.

- Note the answers to the three questions in your Journal and reflect on how you can integrate these into your life.

The part of Heather's life that was out of control presented itself as a fiery dancing symbol and, when she asked these questions, she discovered that it wanted fun, needed respect and offered her abandonment and self-indulgence. She had been pondering these answers for some while, wondering how she could accommodate these requirements, when a friend suggested they go to a Salsa class which had just been started. She hugely enjoyed the classes, the rhythmic energy of the dance and its improvisatory style, and over the course of several months found she had more energy. Her dance provided structure while allowing her to abandon herself to its rhythms and the teacher admired her easy flowing style. Although it took her some time to realise it, the combination of structure and freedom, of control and abandonment, and the respect she gained from her peers, enabled her to take action and to bring more organisation and discipline into her personal life.

Taking action is essential if there is to be change in your life. It is positive, affirmative and confidence-building. If, like Heather, there are parts of your life where you are stuck, then taking action will create change. Taking action is a choice and choosing to act is invigorating. Think back to a time in your life when you did take action. It might have been a small act, like calling the plumber to fix a dripping tap, or a large one like deciding to apply for a job, and remember how great that made you feel. You can feel great again. You can choose to act and, having chosen, you can take action!

10.
Be Flexible

A lack of flexibility is immobilising! Changing from being rigid, uptight and restrained is not impossible. It requires thinking and doing things differently, and then practising it until you are perfect. It is no more of a challenge than physical inflexibility. If you are stiff, get moving!

Inflexible thinking narrows your field of choice. If you think you can do something, you are probably right; if you think you can't do something, again, you are probably right. If you want more choices, then change your thinking and your behaviour, avoiding the temptation to think in the way you have always thought and to do things as you have always done them. The parable of the *Hole In The Road* [42]is a fine example of 'if you do what you've always done, you'll get what you've always got':

> *A man walks down a road and he falls into a hole. The*
> *following day, he walks down the same road and falls in*
> *it again. The next day, the man remembers the hole, but*
> *too late and he falls in again. The day after that, he*
> *knows the hole is there, but even so, he falls in it yet*
> *again. The following day he takes a different road.*

There are three simple things you can do to avoid falling down the same hole day after day:

1. Think More Flexibly

Become aware of when you have a reaction to which you respond almost without thinking, as if you are on auto-pilot. This is rigid thinking. Experiment with thinking the opposite so you are flexible in your thinking, and that way you will widen your variety of responses and broaden the range of choices.

One example: A friend calls and invites you out for lunch.

---

[42] Source unknown

Your auto-response is to say No. You don't know why you say this, but you do, and perhaps afterwards you regret that you did not say Yes. The next time a friend calls, be aware of your tendency to say No to invitations and say 'Yes, thank you, that would be lovely'.

Another example: You sit next to someone who has a bad cold. Your auto-reaction is to think 'I'll get it'. Next time this happens, think instead that you will stay fit and well. Not only are you thinking more flexibly, but you are being positive and you have increased the range of possibilities by 100%!

Thinking flexibly will stop you falling into the hole of always thinking in the same old way about the same old things. If every time you think about the government or your daughter-in-law, the same thoughts come up, experiment with different thoughts such as 'They're doing their best', 'I'm glad I haven't got their job', 'She does the best she can'.

2. Behave With Flexibility

Behaving flexibly will widen your choices in any situation. You don't have to change your life, but you may find that your life does change if you are behaviourally less unbending.

An example: if you always get up, make a cup of tea, go to the bathroom, have breakfast– experiment with changing this routine. OK, getting up will probably have to come first, but try changing the order. Get up, go to the bathroom, make a cup of tea, have breakfast.

Another example: if you have always put your right leg into your trousers / knickers first, change this by putting your left leg in first, making sure you don't fall over!! If you put milk in your tea and then sugar, reverse the order.

A final example: do you always take the same route to

the supermarket? Try-out another itinerary, or another means of getting there (by bike, train, bus, car, on foot).

Being more flexible in your behaviour permits greater choice. If you think there is only one way of doing things, your way, or the right way, then you are likely mistaken. Get into the habit of asking yourself whether there are other options.

3. Embracing Change and Newness

The only thing that is certain is that there will be change. If you doubt this, think about how much in your own life and the external world has changed in the last 20 or 30 years – the internet, the dominance of supermarkets, immigration, multi-culturalism, globalisation. Do your grandchildren wear the same sort of clothes that you wore at their age? Do they speak in the same way? Listen to the same music? Eat the same food? I hope not because they'd be mighty odd if they did!

Impermanence is central to Buddhist teachings. Everything is subject to change and alteration. Life is like a river. Although it gives the impression of continuous flow, it is a succession of different moments which, taken together, appear to be a continuous whole. The river of yesterday is not the river of today. The river now is not the same as the river of 5 seconds or 5 minutes ago.

So with life. It changes constantly. Impermanence and change are undeniable truths of our existence, so you might as well embrace change because it is going to happen anyway.

To successfully embrace change, adopt an attitude of curiosity rather than downright rejection. It simply is not true that all change is bad and that all new things are inherently wrong. Faced with newness begin by assuming an 'isn't that interesting' approach. When your grandson shows you his new mobile phone, be interested, be enthusiastic, ask questions, ask him to show you some of its amazing features; you don't have to buy one (although you might).

The more flexible you are, the less rigid you will be. Being looser in your thinking will have an impact on your feelings and your behaviour. You will slacken the ties that bind you, will feel lighter, and will lighten up.

11.

No Rules

A friend of mine who had been dating on the internet for some time found herself a potential new partner. In telling me about him, she had many thoughts about what was OK and what wasn't, about what she should and shouldn't do. The next day I sent her a copy of my latest best-seller: "New Rules for Relationships" accompanied by the instruction to read it from cover to cover at least once a day and to carry it with her at all times in case of emergency. The book was 20 pages long and, except for the title page, each one was blank. Message: there are no rules!

There are no rules but there is the law of the land, moral codes and common sense. Thomas Edison said, "There are no rules here. We're trying to accomplish something." Rules place limits on possibility, boundaries round opportunities, restrictions on freedom, and they control what you can think, feel and do. If you throw the rules away, then the vista widens, new opportunities and possibilities emerge.

If you choose to live without rules, you will be more dependent on your own resources. You cannot rely on the rulebook or other people to tell you what to do; you have to make up your own mind, decide what you want to do, how you want to do it, and live with the outcomes.

There are no rules about how you should live your life or who you should be. You are free to be whosoever you wish to be, and you are free to live your life as you choose. In her poem, "Warning" (the first line of which is much quoted on birthday cards for anyone over about 10), Jenny Joseph writes of the liberation of ageing:

"When I am an old woman I shall wear purple
With a red hat which doesn't go, and doesn't suit me.
And I shall spend my pension on brandy and summer gloves
And satin sandals, and say we've no money for butter.

I shall sit down on the pavement when I'm tired
And gobble up samples in shops and press alarm bells
And run my stick along the public railings
And make up for the sobriety of my youth.

I shall go out in my slippers in the rain
And pick flowers in other people's gardens
And learn to spit.

You can wear terrible shirts and grow more fat
And eat three pounds of sausages at a go
Or only bread and pickle for a week
And hoard pens and pencils and beer mats and things in boxes.

But now we must have clothes that keep us dry
And pay our rent and not swear in the street
And set a good example for the children.
We must have friends to dinner and read the papers.

But maybe I ought to practice a little now?
So people who know me are not too shocked and surprised
When suddenly I am old, and start to wear purple." [43]

In the same vein, Nadine Stair [44] writes of how she would live her life if she had it over again:

[43] From *Rose in the Afternoon*. Littlehampton Book Services Ltd. 1975. ISBN-13: 978-0460021623

[44] Wikipedia reports that the first known version of the text was authored by American humorist and cartoonist Don Herold and published by the Reader's Digest on October 1953 under the title "I'd Pick More Daisies". http://en.wikipedia.org/wiki/Moments_%28poem%29

"If I had my life to live over, I'd dare to make more mistakes next time. I'd relax. I would limber up. I would be sillier than I have been this trip. I would take fewer things seriously. I would take more chances. I would take more trips. I would climb more mountains and swim more rivers. I would eat more ice cream and less beans. I would perhaps have more actual troubles, but I'd have fewer imaginary ones. You see, I'm one of those people who live sensibly and sanely hour after hour, day after day. Oh, I've had my moments and if I had it to do over again, I'd have more of them. In fact, I'd try to have nothing else. Just moments, one after another, instead of living so many years ahead of each day. I've been one of those persons who never goes anywhere without a thermometer, a hot water bottle, a raincoat, and a parachute. If I had to do it again, I would travel lighter than I have. If I had my life to live over, I would start barefoot earlier in the spring and stay that way later in the fall. I would go to more dances. I would ride more merry-go-rounds. I would pick more daisies."

It may be that eating three pounds of sausages at a go, or picking more daisies does not have any allure for you, but the message is there again: no rules! You are free to create your life in whatever way you want it to be. There may be constraints, of which physical health and money may be among the chief of them, but those apart, who is to say that you can't live however you want? Your children may be shocked or surprised if you take off to live in an ashram for a year, or to walk round the coast of Scotland. Let them be shocked, grant them their surprise.

Life is short. Time is rationed. You have 24 hours in a day, 168 hours in a week and 8,760 hours in a year. If you live to be 100, then from the minute you leap from the womb to the second you breathe your last, you will have 876,000 hours. If you are aged 60 now, you have already expended 525,600 and will have 350,400 left if you live to be 100; 262,800 if you live to be 90; 175,200 if you make it to 80; 87,600 to 70; and 43,800 if

111

you get to 65 and one-third of these will be spent asleep. The clock is ticking – now!

Time then to ditch the rules and to do things differently. Here are a couple of tips about how you might do that:

Rewriting The Rules

1. More Possibility, Less Necessity

If your head is full of words like "must", "must not", "should", "should not", "ought", "ought not", they need to be challenged because they limit your options by applying someone else's rules:

- 'I must eat my 5 a day';

- 'I must not swear';

- 'I should drink 2 litres of water a day';

- 'I shouldn't be so clumsy';

- 'I ought to have so-and-so to dinner';

- 'I ought not to eat bread and pickle for a week'.

These are rules that have been lodged in our head usually by others long departed. Contest these imperatives by asking yourself: "Who says?" and "Supposing I did?"

Become aware of when you are being driven by these injunctions and change the words, using ones such as could, can, might, it's possible, may:

- 'I could eat my 5 a day';

- 'I can choose not to swear';

- 'I might drink 2 litres of water a day';

- 'It is possible to be more careful';

- 'I may have so-and-so to dinner';

- 'I could choose not to eat bread and pickle for a week'.

2. Live Up To Your Own Ideas, Not Other People's

We've all had them, the poison playmates who suck the last drop of energy out of us and leave us feeling depleted and deficient.

J K Rowling described these sort of friends most eloquently in *Harry Potter*;

"Dementors are among the foulest creatures that walk this earth. They infest the darkest, filthiest places, they glory in decay and despair, they drain peace, hope, and happiness out of the air around them... Get too near a Dementor and every good feeling, every happy memory will be sucked out of you."

Someone I know calls the Dementors 'Mood Hoovers'.

Whatever you call them, their effect is the same. Live up to your own ideas, not other people's rules or ideas of how you should or shouldn't live. Confront their negativity, negate it with heartfelt and unfailing enthusiasm. Death to the Dementors! Do not let them win!

Identify the people in your life who are your Dementors and ditch them.

Choosing to live a life without rules is liberating, but it is not a life without responsibility. However you choose to live, your aim could be to balance the freedom you have with responsibility to yourself and to others.

12.
Be Resilient

Humpty Dumpty sat on a wall
Humpty Dumpty had a great fall
All the king's horses and all the King's men
Couldn't put Humpty together again

Whoever or whatever Humpty Dumpty was, one thing is certain, he lacked resilience; otherwise he would have picked himself up, put himself together again and climbed back onto the wall. To be resilient is to have the capability of bouncing back in the face of setbacks; to let the water flow off the duck's back, to be strong enough to handle the slings and arrows of outrageous fortune, to be unbroken by the sticks and stones, and to be able to return to a state of normal functioning, unimpaired.

Resilience is not about being so armour-plated that your emotional responses are shut down to the extent that nothing can penetrate your armour; it is about having emotional bounce! This elasticity can be learned and developed, and, as you will see, you have already learned some of these skills in earlier chapters:

12 Ways To Be Resilient

1. You Have A Choice

When facing misfortunes, you have a choice as to how you respond. Remember how Victor Frankl emphasised that even in the concentration camps, the one remaining freedom was to 'choose one's attitude in any given set of circumstances'.

2. Let Go

You do not have to hang on to the discomfort or pain of your troubles. You can choose non-attachment – recognising that there is a problem, but not getting sucked into it so that it saps your energy. You can do this by returning to the exercise where you dumped old ways of thinking and feeling at the bottom of sea (see *Dumping The Old* in Chapter 4); or by choosing to live in the present, or by being appreciative of what you do have rather than bemoaning your lack.

3. Accept What Is

Accepting adversity as it is starves it of energy and curtails its power. Should you choose to be overwhelmed by difficulties, you will be feeding your anxiety. You will find the hard times you are passing through more acceptable if you choose to bless the obstacle and move on.

4. Be grateful

The hurdle you are facing is most likely indicating that there is something in your life, your attitude or your thinking that you need to change. If you are able to view this as feedback rather than failure, you will be open to learning the lesson it is trying to teach you. Take the learning from the experience, be grateful for the opportunity you have been given and move on.

5. Be Positive

Re-read Chapter 7 so that you can dispute what may be a negative spin you have put on an event; challenge the voice in your head; reframe the experience in a different context; explore the part of you which is being negative or self-critical.

Aim too to find a positive aspect to whatever befalls you. A crisis is an opportunity to grow and develop. A chance to move away from something which is not working, and to move towards something which works better.

6. Be realistic

Keep the setback in proportion by questioning your thinking. Are you over-egging the pudding, giving undue weight to events, are your reactions proportionate to the severity of the obstacle, are you expecting too much of yourself or others, are you resisting an acceptance of events as they really are?

7. Take Action

Do something and do it now! Start work immediately on taking steps to resolve the issue. You may not be able to sort it out in one easy move, but action will stop you getting stuck, will reduce your anxiety and allow you to move on.

As I was writing this, a friend called to say some tiles had slipped off her roof and she was feeling thoroughly miserable about it. I asked if she had called a roofer. She hadn't. She called back later to say that someone was coming round first thing in the morning to look at the problem and she was feeling better already.

You do not have to submissively accept misfortune - acceptance is not an act of passivity, but one of action (Hamlet questioned "Whether 'tis nobler in the mind to suffer the slings and arrows of outrageous fortune, or to take arms against a sea of troubles, and by opposing end them?") [45] It may be a myth that suffering is noble, but it is also unnecessary if the sea of troubles can be opposed and subdued.

I repeat Susan Jeffers's statement: "Action is very positive and very powerful."

8. Be Flexible

It may be that you are experiencing challenges in your life as a result of being too rigid in your thinking or behaviour. Are you thinking about or doing things in the same old way time after time, bound by the same old rules? If so, you could maybe benefit from releasing your tight hold on your life and experimenting with new, more

---

[45] Shakespeare, William. *Hamlet.* Act 3, Scene 1.

117

flexible thoughts and ways of doing things.

9. Keep Going

Don't give up! Persevere and be persistent, finding the inner strength to keep going.

10. Maintain Your Sense of Humour

If you can laugh at the twists and turns of life (especially if you are over-sensitive to criticism), you will feel better and will have a lighter, more positive view of circumstances.

11. Become The Observer

Step back from the situation and observe what is happening from a position of neutrality. Many a time things will go wrong and you do not need to have a reaction or to get involved; instead you can choose to be non-attached and silently observe the comedy of your life.

12. Ask for Support

If you need practical or emotional help, then ask for it. As mentioned before, people are keen to lend a hand as long as you are clear about your needs.

A reservoir of inner strength will ensure that you have a ready supply of inner bounce. Inner strength comes from having a strong Will (see Chapter 3) and the exercise below will help you to develop strong Will:

Developing Inner Strength

• Make yourself comfortable and ensure you are warm. Close your eyes.

• Bring to mind a clear image of yourself as if you are watching yourself in a movie from a seat in the cinema. See yourself on the screen *being in possession* of a strong Will; see yourself walking with a firm and determined step, acting in every situation with decision, focused intention, and persistence; see yourself successfully resisting any attempt at intimidation and enticement. Imagine that a steel rod is being inserted painlessly into your spine and notice the effect of this on your body.

• Imagine you are stepping into the screen and into your own body. This time <u>experience</u> how it is to *be in possession* of a strong will; to walk with a firm and determined step, to act in every situation with decisiveness, focused intention, and persistence; to successfully resist any attempt at intimidation and enticement. Feel the strengthening power of the steel rod in your spine.

• Allow the image to fade, open your eyes and return to the room.

The next stage is to go out into the world and *act as if* you do indeed have strong Will. You can walk firmly and determinedly; you can be decisive, focused and persistent, and you can successfully resist distractions of any kind. And while you are acting as if you have a strong Will, you can internalise (and further strengthen) the feelings that go with it. You can notice how you really do **feel to be** strong, firm, determined, decisive, intent, persistent, and unwavering.

You have developed resilience and inner strength. You now have the ability to bounce back from the strains and stresses of life and jump back on the wall.

Amazing Ageing

Developing A Spiritual Life

13.
A Spiritual Journey

Why would you want to undertake a spiritual journey or to live a spiritual life? It is my belief that if we do not consciously and consistently focus on the spiritual part of ourselves, we will never experience the kind of joy, satisfaction and connectedness we are all seeking. There will be something missing.

The benefits of you developing a spiritual life as you age are:

- You will more easily develop new qualities, attitudes and behaviours. As your inner life grows, so you will strengthen the qualities of choice, acceptance, letting go, gratitude, positivity, realism, action, flexibility, resilience, and living free from the constraint of rules.
- You will loosen the grip of fear as your inner spiritual life develops. Fear lies at the root of many of our difficulties.
- You will develop detachment and the desires and cravings which are the seeds of suffering will wither and perish.
- You will be more resilient to changes in outside circumstances.
- You will be able to rise above frustration, disappointment, regrets, resentments and negative feelings.
- You will feel stronger and more powerful.
- You will feel safer and more secure.
- Your intuition will be sharper.
- You will be happier and have greater peace of mind.

A spiritual journey can be described as being on a path toward a higher state of awareness, of realising your potential, and tapping into your wisdom. I emphasize that, even though there may be a connection, spirituality is **not** religion and can be separate from it. Being "spiritual" is not necessarily about going to church but involves empathic understanding, altruistic love, wisdom, realisation of human potential, creativity, the appreciation of beauty, a sense of responsibility, mystical or peak experiences, a sense of oneness with the universe.

There are some common themes associated with a spiritual quest:

- A journey of self-discovery, learning who you are and what you may be; Nietzsche, foreshadowing Victor Frankl and his experience in the concentration camps, wrote that "He who has a why to live can bear almost any how."[46]
- A call to go beyond your present limitations which may include being open-minded and questioning your current beliefs.
- Connection with yourself, others and the world around you.
- Finding meaning, purpose and direction in your life, even when, like Roberto Assagioli, you are in prison. This is finding your own unique calling or mission in life. The Hero's Journey, given in Appendix D, is often used as an example of a spiritual journey from the known to the unknown world with the hero returning to the known transformed.
- The existence of a higher power whether it be of a religious origin, nature, or some unknown force.

All spiritual searches are journeys which seek to liberate the universal wisdom within you (sometimes called consciousness) and this might be achieved through transcendence and immanence:

1. Transcendence is when a new vision of life becomes apparent (this is what happens to The Hero when he leaves his known, everyday world and journeys into the "region of supernatural wonder"). A stereotypical example is the person who, like The Hero, withdraws

---

[46] Friedrich Nietzsche. *Twilight Of The Idols.* 1888

from the world to a cave or mountain top to meditate until he gains enlightenment. It is not for everybody.

2. Immanence is living out the resulting transformation in the everyday world. The Hero, transformed by the trials of his journey, returns to the everyday world and puts to use everything he has learned, to the benefit of others.

The transcendent and the immanent came together most beautifully in Eileen Caddy, who died in 2006 aged 89. Eileen was a spiritual teacher and author, best known as one of the founders of the Findhorn Foundation community near the village of Findhorn in northeast Scotland which she started in 1962 with her then husband Peter Caddy and their friend Dorothy Maclean. After a traumatic end to her first marriage, Eileen heard in meditation the 'voice of God' which said: "Be still and know that I am God." Somewhat alarmed she took this to be symptomatic of a nervous breakdown. Later she lived her own life and gave guidance to the community she had established by listening daily to the voice of "the God within us all".

Eileen was a remarkable person and was firmly of the view that spirituality was of little value unless it was lived out in words and actions in the world. The antithesis of the mountain top guru, Eileen for many years meditated early in the morning in all weathers in the outside lavatory at Findhorn, which was the one place she could find peace and quiet!

All of this may give you the impression that spiritual development is strenuous, that you have to be a special type of person or go to a special place. Well, you are special person, and, yes, a spiritual journey can be very testing and hugely rewarding, and you can do it anywhere (even in an outside loo). You can do it anywhere because the journey is within, a voyage to your true self. The self you know, your personality, is limited because it defines itself in terms of your physical body, your possessions, your role in society and how others see you. This is false; it is a facade behind which lies your true self. To know your true self, you choose first to connect with your inner guide or soul (in Eileen Caddy's words "the God within us all") who will guard you, guide you and protect you on your journey through life.

First though read this short story.[47]

> One day, according to an Eastern story, the gods decided to create the universe. After they had created all the things which gods usually create - stars, sun, moon, seas, plants, animals, they got round to creating human beings and, finally, Truth. This was problematic, because while they wanted the humans to have access to Truth, they didn't want them to find it too easily.
> "Let's put Truth on top of the highest mountain," said one. "Certainly it will be hard to find it there."
> "Let's put it on the farthest star," said another.
> "Let's hide it in the darkest and deepest of abysses."
> "Let's conceal it on the secret side of the moon."
> At the end the wisest and most ancient god said, "No, we will hide Truth inside the very heart of human beings. In this way they will look for it all over the universe, without being aware of having it inside themselves all the time."

And that is what they did! The truth, your access point to the universal wisdom, is within you.

Before you go and find your inner guide, let's make some preparations for the journey, by asking yourself some questions. You can record these and your answers in your Journal.

Preparation For A Spiritual Journey

These questions will test and challenge your current beliefs, reveal gaps in your knowledge, and will also stretch your mind by pushing you to think beyond your

---

[47] Adapted from *What we may be*, Piero Ferrucci. (Turnstone Press, 1989). p. 143.

126

normal comfort zone:

- Who are the most important people in my life?

- How have they affected me?

- With whom do I feel most comfortable?

- What is about this person that means I am comfortable with them?

- What is my ideal way of living my life?

- What would my life be like if money didn't matter?

- What would I like my life to be in 10 years?

- What goals do I have for the coming year? the next five years?

- How can I avoid living a stagnant life?

- Do things happen for a reason?

- What do I believe?

- What is the purpose of my life?

- What specific experiences have shaped my beliefs?

- Am I a good person?

- In what way am I a good person?

- What qualities do I need to develop to become a good person?

Right! You are now ready to meet your inner guide. This is your inner wisdom which will guard you, guide you and protect you on life's journey.

Meeting Your Inner Guide

- Make yourself comfortable and ensure you are warm. Close your eyes.

- Visualise yourself going to a peaceful place such as a meadow on a warm, sunny day. Visualise this place as fully as you can - seeing what you see, hearing what you hear and feeling what you feel. Take time to see the grass and the flowers, to hear the birds and the sounds of nature, to feel calm and serene.

- Look around and you see a mountain. Decide to climb the mountain.

- Begin your journey by entering a forest. Smell the scent of the pine trees, and sense the cool, dark, atmosphere.

- Leave the forest, going out into warmth and sunlight again, and begin your ascent of the mountain. Feel the energy required to walk uphill, the muscular effort which it takes.

- Approaching the top of the mountain notice how it is rocky and that the ascent is becoming harder. The air is fresher and there is complete silence.

- At the top of the mountain you go into cloud and you are enveloped in mist.

- Suddenly the mist clears and you can see the sun and the blue sky, everything is brighter, and the final ascent is easier.

- Once at the very top, you are on a vast plateau, the silence is total, the sky is the very deepest blue.

- Far off you see someone. It is a person who is wise and loving, ready to listen to what you have to say and to tell you what you want to know. Imagine this person, who is your inner guide, in as much detail as you can. However if your guide looks like a critical, judgmental person, gently thank them and ask them to send your inner guide to you.

- Walk towards each other slowly, feeling the presence

of this wise person. You see this person's face and smile, and you feel yourself wrapped in a loving warmth.

- Face each other and look into this person's eyes.

- Thank your inner guide for coming.

- You have the opportunity to ask your inner guide any questions you may have. You may want to ask one or more of the questions you wrestled with in the previous section. There is no need to rush this, so wait patiently for an answer. If there is no answer, trust that it will appear at another time.

- Once you feel you are complete, thank your inner guide for being with you and watch them go away as you descend the mountain slowly, pass once more through the forest and return to the meadow. Open your eyes and return to normal waking consciousness.

Expanding Your Inner World

Now that you have met your inner guide, you can begin to live out what you have discovered in the world. Here are some suggestions.

- ***Community Service***
Do some volunteering in your community. This will help you to develop compassion and you will get a better understanding of how and where you fit into the world. You will also learn that other people's experience and circumstances are different from your own.

- ***Talk to others***
Use the questions you considered in preparation for your spiritual journey and talk to sympathetic friends, family, or peers about them. It is unwise to talk about your inner guide and the guidance you receive to people who, for whatever reason, would be indifferent, derisive or

disobliging. Talking can help you to sort out those things you may not be able to work out on your own. You can test out your new way of thinking and behaving and get support.

- ### *Yoga*

There are many benefits to practicing Yoga – it works on the physical body, so you gain strength, flexibility and ease of movement as well as improving physiological functions such as your breathing, your circulation, your digestive system, your endocrine system, your lymphatic system. Mentally you will become more focused and have greater awareness of how you move in relation to the rest of your life.

- ### *Gratitude*

Gratitude was covered earlier in the book, nevertheless being grateful and thankful are important components of living a more spiritual, ethical life. In your Journal write a list of things that make you feel good and refer to it when you are not feeling so great. Listen to inspirational music or CDs of motivating talks. Do the Evening Review (see Chapter 6) on a daily basis.

As well as living out your inner life in the world, you can strengthen your communication and contact with your inner guide.

Writing A Letter To Your Inner Guide

- As always, sit where you are comfortable and allow yourself to sink into a calm relaxed state.

- You are writing to your inner guide. What do you want to say to him or her? What do you want to ask? On what issues would you like guidance? [It might be that you want some guidance on some issues related to ageing which you find challenging, or it may be something else].

- There is no right or wrong way of doing this. Write what you feel and what your hand guides you to write, go with your thoughts, with what feels right for you.

- Once you are complete, close your Journal and do something else.

- When it feels appropriate, return to your Journal and write a reply from your inner guide.

- Once you are finished, close your Journal and do something different.

- When you come back to your Journal reflect from a dispassionate observer position on your letter and the reply it elicited.

- Record any thoughts or feelings it evokes.

Living A Good Life

Challenge yourself to live a good life – to live out and make concrete in your actions the tenets and guidance of your inner guide – and to be a more wholesome person. Most societies and religions have a moral code, Islam, Judaism, Christianity and the essence of these is incorporated in formal legal codes and modes of behaviour which vary from country to country.

The fundamental moral code of Buddhism is The Five Precepts - or Negative Virtues – which may not be familiar to you. The Five Precepts are balanced by and correspond to The Five Ennobling Virtues. I have chosen to present both ends of the see-saw simultaneously – the Precept and the Virtue together. I have also chosen to interpret them in a modern context so that they are relevant to living in today's world; to have interpreted them literally and as written would be doctrinaire and fall into the trap of some adherents to dogma which live to the very letter codes written for a different time.

Being mindful of my unbending rule that 'there are no rules', The Precepts can be taken as recommendations not as commandments. You are encouraged to reflect upon them and, if you think it appropriate, to apply them in the manner most suitable for you – it is the spirit of the precepts and not the text that counts.

Because The Precepts are unfamiliar you will read them with fresh eyes and they will stimulate fresh thinking.

1. Not Taking Life, Not Harming; And Acting With Loving Kindness

Be conscious of when you are hurting or being cruel to others (including plants and animals) not just in what you do but in what you think or for what you wish. Act with kindness and compassion, being alert and responsive to the needs of others, helping others to be more human and compassionate themselves. If your thoughts about yourself or other people are harsh and judgmental use the words of the Loving Kindness meditation[48]: "May you be well, may you be happy, may you be free from suffering."

2. Not Taking The Not Given; And Acting With Generosity

While this refers to stealing of any kind, it subtly includes taking anything unless we know it has been freely given – most obviously this would cover acquiring anything by extortion or deception but also less obviously (as a friend of mine used to do) taking without permission – it was her habit to take food from an hotel's breakfast buffet to eat at lunchtime. Sure, the food was available, some would certainly go to waste, and the cost, no doubt, had been accounted for in the bill. But this is to miss the point. She was removing the food which was being offered to guests at breakfast,

---

[48] "The Metta Bhavana, or Development of Loving Kindness, practice is one of the most ancient forms of Buddhist practice, one that has been passed down in an unbroken line for over 2,500 years." Source: http://www.wildmind.org/metta

concealing it in her handbag, and the hotel had not expressly given its consent to people taking goodies for their lunch as well. Such behaviour is theft. So too is 'borrowing' things from other people without their permission. If your son comes home for the weekend and, without asking, leaves his laundry for you to do in time for his next visit, this is theft of your time.

This precept encourages us not to exploit other people, by following it we can be more conscious about where and by whom our clothes are made; where the coffee comes from and how well rewarded the growers are.

The ennobling virtue suggests that we be generous and giving rather than miserly and grabbing. Consider when you are generous and with what you are generous. With money? With food? With time? With words of encouragement and compassion? With random acts of kindness?

3. To Abstain From Sexual Misconduct; And To Seek Stillness And Contentment.

This precept is capable of misinterpretation as it was written in the context of another country and a different age. While sex is pleasurable, it is not to be overvalued. With ageing, the strong sexual drives of youth fade, but there is still the possibility of sexual behaviour which involves physical and mental harm to others, is disrespectful to others and devalues personal relationships. What is your own response to internet porn, or prostitution, or child prostitution, or sex trafficking, or sex tourism? At what point for you does flirting become infidelity?

The ennobling virtue calls us to be respectful to others, to value personal relationships and to seek stillness and contentment. Being contented is not a sterile, emotionally arid state; rather it is a tranquil place where our intentions and our pleasures can be enriching and satisfying. If during a long marriage or relationship the sexual urge diminishes, you can find contentment in the companionship and friendship of your partner, in the pleasures of being together and sharing things with each other.

4. To Abstain From Telling Falsehoods; And To Communicate Truthfully.

Telling falsehoods encompasses telling lies, hypocrisy, making a promise without intending to keep it, exaggeration, sarcasm, insults, gossip, and being deceitful. Do any of these words surprise you?

To communicate truthfully is a significant challenge. I was once on a training course on which someone committed to being truthful for 24 hours; the following day she reported that she had failed, not because she had not been truthful, but because she had withheld a response or been oblique when she thought she might hurt someone else. The balance is to be found in being authentic and acting with loving kindness. Some situations, which are unpalatable and uncomfortable, require that the truth be told – "You're fired", "I've fallen in love with someone else", "We've run out of money" – but this can be done with kindness and compassion. At other, less fraught, times it is possible to be truthful and kind by speaking positively and appreciatively.

Of all the words in the first sentence of this section I wonder which stood out for you? I would hazard it might be gossip. I have worked in office environments where gossip has been the dominant activity, eclipsing the importance of the task in hand. I have been in social situations where people who have not been present have been vilified. How best to react? One option is to be a silent non-participant. Another, demanding courage, is to say that you have many faults of your own and you prefer not to dwell on the shortcomings of others.

5. To Abstain From Intoxicants; And To Act With Mindfulness.

This may seem harsh for societies where alcohol is not just acceptable, but is part of the social currency. The reasoning

134

which lies behind the precept has value regardless. Alcohol is expensive and debatably a waste of money, it dulls strong feelings, may lead to domestic violence, is injurious to health, can be a source of shame and humiliation, and leads to loss of physical, mental and emotional self-control. As you age, your tolerance for alcohol reduces – you simply cannot drink as much in your 80s as you did at 18. Alcoholism is an illness which has often terrible consequences for all involved.

It has been argued that getting intoxicated or addicted to sex or shopping is 'filling the hole' rather than 'feeling whole' – what Roberto Assagioli called "Divine Homesickness", the feeling that something is missing from your life (but you don't know what), a sense of existential emptiness or intense loneliness accompanied by a desire for something which is other and beyond. Assagioli believed also that every human contains an inner impulse to integration, wholeness and actualisation.

Mindfulness, a deceptively 'small word' for an exacting and demanding way of being, presses us to be consciously aware (mindful) of our thoughts, our feelings, our actions and behaviour, and to be watchful of our effect on others and the world. As the vogue phrase would have it, this is a 'big ask', but then the Divine Homecoming is not be found in a bottle, a syringe, or Harvey Nichols.

Developing Mindfulness

Mindfulness is a smallish word with a big meaning. Jon Kabat-Zinn[49], an authority on mindfulness, defines it as: "Paying attention in a particular way, on purpose, in the present moment, and non-judgmentally." Mindfulness is a conscious and purposeful direction of your attention and awareness. When you are eating, you may be aware that you are eating but not mindful of it; your mind may be occupied with hundreds of other things such as talking to your friend, thinking about what you

---

[49] Professor of Medicine Emeritus and founding director of the Stress Reduction Clinic and the Centre for Mindfulness in Medicine, Health Care, and Society at the University of Massachusetts Medical School.

are going to do after you have eaten, listening to the radio or watching TV, almost anything except eating!

When you are mindful of eating, you would be intentionally aware of the process of eating, of taking food from the plate to your mouth, the sensation of chewing the food and swallowing it, of the smells, tastes and flavours. If your mind wanders, you would gently bring it back to eating.

Mindfulness is about giving your attention to what is going on right now; not to what happened in the past or what might happen in the future. The one moment to which you can give your attention is the present – the one it is most tempting to avoid! Mindfulness is non-judgmental; you are noticing the action of eating and the taste of the food but you are not judging it. In keeping your mind focused, you handicap its attempts to wander off on its own. Left to wander, your mind can go off in futile directions, revisiting old thoughts and negative feelings and thereby reinforcing them.

As you develop mindfulness, you will be more able to:
- Be fully present, in the here and now;
- Increase self-awareness;
- Learn the distinction between you and your thoughts;
- Learn that thoughts and feelings come and go like clouds in the sky;
- Cope with unpleasant old thoughts and negative feelings safely;
- Be aware of what you're avoiding;
- Become more connected to yourself, to others and to the world around you;
- Be more balanced, calm and peaceful.

Mindfulness is not a state which can be achieved in a single bound! There are four steps you can take which will get you to the first floor, if not higher.

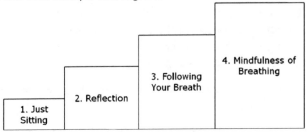

1. Just sitting

This is a meditation practice which has no specific focus. Sit comfortably and quietly, making sure that you will be warm as your body cools down (which it will). Thoughts will come in and out of your mind, sounds will intrude from the outside; allow this to happen, but do not hang on to any thought or sound which comes. Just let it pass like a cloud in the sky.

Some thoughts will be sticky. You may suddenly remember something you have committed to do, or forgotten to do. Let it float by. You can attend to whatever needs to be done later. You do not have to do it now.

Start by doing this for a few minutes and then build up to just sitting for 10 or 15 minutes. It is harder than it sounds because you will be accustomed to hanging onto thoughts like a dog worrying a bone. Just sitting is great for not getting attached to whatever comes into your mind. Noticing it and then letting it go.

When you are finished, spend time reflecting on what you have done. How easy did you find it? How active was your mind? Were you surprised by the torrent of thoughts which passed by? Were you surprised by the variety of thoughts you had?

You can record your reflections in your Journal.

2. Reflection

In this step you do focus on something - a quality which you wish to develop within yourself. The list from which you might choose is endless, but, for the sake of simplicity, let's choose simplicity!

Sit comfortably, making sure that you will be warm. Take a few breaths.

Now think about the idea of SIMPLICITY. Jot down in your Journal the ideas that come.

Recognise the value and benefits of SIMPLICITY.

Appreciate SIMPLICITY and what it offers you in your busy, thought-crowded life.

Be grateful for SIMPLICITY.

Invite SIMPLICITY into your life.

Take on the physical attitude of SIMPLICITY.

Allow SIMPLICITY to express itself on your face and in your body.

Evoke the quality of SIMPLICITY by closing your eyes and imagining yourself in a calm and peaceful place. Repeat the word SIMPLICITY several times and as you do so allow SIMPLICITY to infuse you until you reach a point where you feel to become SIMPLICITY.

Imagine yourself going about your daily life, bringing to mind those parts of your life which are complicated or confusing, and see and feel yourself doing things calmly and simply. Make a pact with yourself to bring SIMPLICITY more and more into your life.

Design a Post-It note with the word SIMPLICITY on it and place it somewhere where you will see it during the day. Whenever you see it, bring to mind the feeling of

SIMPLICITY.

You can record your reflections in your Journal.

3. Following Your Breath

Sit with your back straight, but not so straight you are uncomfortable, making sure that you are warm. Close your eyes, allow your body to relax, enough to feel relaxed but not so much that you immediately fall into a deep sleep. Breathe naturally without forcing anything.

Become aware of your breathing, noticing the feeling of your breath coming in and out, observe the difference between your in-breath and your out-breath. If your mind goes off on a journey of its own, gently bring your attention back to your breathing.

Start by doing this for a few minutes and then build up to following your breath for 10 or 15 minutes.

When you are finished, spend time reflecting on what you have done. How easy did you find it? How active was your mind? How easy was it to focus on your breathing? Did you begin to nod off or did you stay observant? Were there any recurring thoughts that just would not go away?

You can record your reflections in your Journal.

4. Mindfulness Of Breathing

Posture

For a beginner, the recommended posture is to sit on an office or dining-room chair. You do not have to hold an upright posture if that is uncomfortable for you as it will be distracting. Be gentle with yourself!

Relaxation

Before the meditation begins you should relax your body.

Make sure that you will be warm, comfortable and

undisturbed. Wrap yourself in a light blanket to keep yourself warm. Let any sounds inside or outside the room just float by like clouds in the sky.

Make sure both your feet are flat on the floor and your hands sit loosely in your lap.

First breathe out to empty your lungs and then breathe in to the slow count of 4, hold for the count of 2 and breathe out for the count of 6, pause for the count of 2 and then repeat 5 times. Set up a rhythm of breathing: In -2 - 3 - 4, Hold - 2, Out - 2 - 3 - 4 - 5 - 6, Pause - 2, etc.

Now breathe normally, noticing your stomach rise as you breathe in and fall as you breathe out. Allow your body to sink into the chair and feel yourself becoming heavy.

Imagine a warm golden light flowing down into and over:

 - the top of your head, forehead, eyes, ears, nose, cheeks, and mouth. Keeping your mouth closed, allow your jaw to sag. Feel the tension around your jaw flowing away.

- the back of your skull, neck and shoulders.

- your upper arms, elbows, lower arms, wrists, hands, down to the tips of your fingers.

- your chest, the area round your heart, your stomach, your hips.

- your back, your buttocks and your pelvis.

- your thighs, your knees, your calves, your ankles, your feet, down to the tips of your toes.

Feel this warm golden light flowing into and over your whole body, from the top of your head down into your fingers and right down to your toes.

Imagine your body is sinking deeper and deeper into the chair and that you are limp and relaxed like a rag doll.

Notice any areas of tension in your body and allow the tension to just flow away through your fingers or toes, down into the floor, deep down into the earth. You body is now relaxed.

Stage 1

Begin counting silently in your head after every out-breath:

Breathe	in	–	breathe	out	–	1
Breathe	in	–	breathe	out	–	2
Breathe	in	–	breathe	out	–	3
Breathe	in	–	breathe	out	–	4
Breathe	in	–	breathe	out	–	5

... etc. until you reach ten. Once you get to ten, start again at one. Do this for 5 minutes. If your mind wanders off, and it will, bring yourself gently back to the counting, starting at 1 again and notice your breathing.

Be aware of letting go, of your body relaxing; and, as your body relaxes, of your mind relaxing.

Stage 2

This is similar to Stage 1, but this time you count just before each inhalation.

So this time, the pattern is like this:

Begin counting silently in your head before every in-breath:

1	–	Breathe	in	–	breathe	out
2	–	Breathe	in	–	breathe	out
3	–	Breathe	in	–	breathe	out
4	–	Breathe	in	–	breathe	out
5	–	Breathe	in	–	breathe	out

... etc. until you reach ten. Once you get to ten, start again at one.

This time be aware of the upward impulse, feel your body expanding and energy coming in with each in-breath. You may feel brighter and more alert.

Stage 3

At this stage, stop the counting, and simply breathe in and out, noticing when you change from an in-breath to an out-breath. Experience your breathing as a loop rather than an in-breath followed by an out-breath.

Stage 4

In the last stage, the aim is to narrow the focus and to become more aware of subtle sensations. This will help to focus concentration and will produce a deep level of calm.

Become aware of where the breath first comes into your nostrils and of the sensation of the breath as it passes over your upper lip.

I met Stuart in a personal development group. He was 59 and he enthusiastically disclosed to the group that he had been a hell raiser in the past and that his favourite word used to be excess. He had drunk heavily, had enjoyed multiple wives and mistresses, sired many children, and had rested only when he lost consciousness. A few years previously, swerving to avoid a cat running across the road, he had come off his motorbike. His left arm had been mangled in the rear wheel and he had left most of his face on the road. It was, he said, "the crisis that was waiting for me". Aware that he would be spending months in hospital, he resolved to understand why this accident ("my tiny wee blessing" as he called it) had happened to him and what, if anything, was the meaning of it all.

Stuart began by writing on lined Basildon Bond to 'god with a small g' (he didn't 'do God') demanding an explanation. Either the reply was lost in the post or god was unimpressed by his stationery, so he tried contacting his inner wisdom through meditation and visualisation. His inner guide was more polite than the god with a small g and he received a reply, which was that he was to visit schools and youth clubs and point out the dangers of motorbikes - "as if the dangers weren't written all over my face". This had developed and he was now working with disaffected teenagers whose fathers were absent. "Ironic isn't it?" he said, "I've more children than I can count on the fingers of my one hand. I love these kids, I love my work. Every day I thank my soul for that damned cat and for the fact I found my life purpose on the A6 outside Buxton."

Physical pain, life crises, abject failure can be catalysts for a spiritual awakening. Stuart, like Humpty Dumpty, fell off one heck of a high wall and only he could put himself back together again and find that he had changed in the process. What is so heart-warming about Stuart's story is not just the extent of his transformation, but that he got in touch with his humanity and his unqualified love for others. He is by no means surrounded by an aura of holiness, but, like the Skin Horse, Stuart is very, very real:

> *"You become. It takes a long time... generally, by the time you are Real, most of your hair has been loved off, and your eyes drop out and you get loose in the joints and very shabby. But these things don't matter at all, because once you are Real you can't be ugly, except to people who don't understand."*[50]

Not all spiritual journeys have to be like Stuart's; his was extreme. Sometimes the quest to live a more spiritual life, a life where you are more in touch with what is authentic and real begins with the niggling question 'Is this all there is?'

You will begin your spiritual journey in your own way and in your own time. Once it has begun you will notice the benefits as you connect with your inner guide and discover the deep calm reservoir of empathic understanding, altruistic love, wisdom, human potential, creativity, and have a sense of oneness with the universe. Never again need you be, or feel, alone.

---

[50] Williams, Margery. *The Velveteen Rabbit.* Running Press, US. !996.

Amazing Ageing

Alone But Not Lonely

14.
Alone But Not Lonely

It is estimated that in the UK 34 per cent of households have only one person living in them; out of every three houses in your area, one of them will be occupied by a person living alone. In some areas, the incidence may be higher. Half of all people aged 75 and over live alone, and 1 in 10 people aged 65 or over say they always or often feel, or are, lonely – that's just over a million people. Buried within the enormity of these figures there are some small shoots of encouragement. One optimistic interpretation is that living alone does not have to mean that you are lonely. What matters is not so much whether you live alone, but whether you **feel** lonely.

Feeling lonely is damaging to your physical and psychological wellbeing. In March 2012, the Campaign To End Loneliness held a summit at which Paul Burstow MP, who was at that time the Care Services Minister, said "We are on the verge of, if not already living through, an epidemic of loneliness and if we do not start to take action it will have huge consequences for individuals and for our health and social care systems." [51]

Research conducted by Professor John Cacioppo of the University of Chicago and presented to the conference of the American Association for the Advancement of Science in 2009 showed that "loneliness can cause:

- raised blood pressure;
- an increase in your level of stress and cortisol production;
- a negative impact on your immune system;
- an inability to sleep well;
- an increased level of depression and anxiety;

---

[51] http://www.campaigntoendloneliness.org.uk/wp-content/uploads/downloads/2012/03/15.03.12-Summit-on-Tackling-Loneliness-Report.pdf

- an increased risk of developing Alzheimer's Disease;
- a reduction in your will to exercise;
- an increase in your cravings for comforting foods high in processed carbohydrates;
- an increase in consumption of calories, alcohol or drugs both legal and illegal;
- a feeling of sadness that feeds upon itself, causing even more isolation and an even greater sense of loneliness." [52]

According to Dr. Cacioppo, "health-wise, the difference between a lonely person and a popular person was akin to a smoker and a non-smoker. That stunned all of us, myself and all my colleagues in terms of the effects it had. It shows just how powerful it is." [53]

What Is Loneliness?

The Campaign To End Loneliness (CEL) describes loneliness as being "a psychological state, an emotional response to a perceived gap between the amount of personal contact an individual wants and the amount they have. It is clearly linked to, but distinct from, the objective state of isolation."[54]

I hypothesize that there are two types of loneliness:

1. Interpersonal Loneliness, described by Robert Weiss, a US sociologist,[55] as being either Emotional Loneliness ("the absence of a significant other with whom a close emotional attachment is formed, e.g. a

---

[52] http://www.healthhabits.ca/2009/02/16/loneliness-worse-for-your-health-than-smoking-and-obesity/

[53] http://www.healthhabits.ca/2009/02/16/loneliness-worse-for-your-health-than-smoking-and-obesity/

[54] Safeguarding the convoy A call to action from the Campaign to End Loneliness.

[55] Weiss, R. (1975) Loneliness: The Experience of Emotional and Social Isolation Cambridge, MA: The MIT Press.

partner or best friend") or Social Loneliness ("the absence of a social network consisting of a wide or broad group of friends, neighbours and colleagues"). The Interpersonal Loner feels the <u>absence or lack</u> of other people, and, unless you are innately lonely, this usually but not always coincides with getting older.

2. Innate Loneliness is of a different order. It is not the lack of other people, but the feeling that even when you are with someone you love or in a crowd you are still lonely. The Innate Loner is typically someone who had negative or critical parents such that s/he was unable to form secure and loving attachments in childhood or someone who has had a history of loss and trauma. Such early experiences become innate or hard-wired and provide the lifelong context of the Innate Loner's emotional life. This grey and lonely backdrop colours or fails to colour their relationships with others, so that, even when surrounded by people, they feel alone.

Ken is an Innate Loner: in 1932, the year he was born, his family of origin consisted of his father (his second marriage), his mother (her first) and three children, aged 16 to 12, from his father's first marriage. He was the replacement child for a boy, Donald, who had died within days of his birth. At the age of four, Ken's half-sister, who had been the focus of his life and, in practice, his primary caregiver was sent away by her father. This was never spoken of and never explained. The effect on Ken was devastating. His sense is that he changed from being a happy carefree child to being anxious and withdrawn. He was sent away to boarding school where he was teased and bullied. He came to the only conclusion possible – he was unlovable.

As a child Ken felt unloved, unwanted, unattached and misunderstood. In his twenties he was overwhelmingly depressed. He sought solace in alcohol and frequent anonymous

149

sexual encounters. He formed unsuitable emotional attachments and was enormously needy. Now, aged 80, he is alone, but not lonely. He can form good friendships and he has many friends. He is liked and respected in the small town where lives. He admits that he has consciously and deliberately made himself agreeable.

Ken's interpretation of his early life is that he was the focus of his parents' hopes and the repository of their grief at the death of Donald, that he was a stand-in and that he could never be good enough or perfect enough. He was not and could not be Donald. Ken says "If I allow myself, I can feel to be an outsider, the little boy shut out in the cold peering in through the window at the party within. I can feel to be cut out of the action and excluded from the dance at the centre of things."

This feeling of being an outsider is a state of mind and Ken has conscientiously worked to modify this state so that life is bearable, so that it can even be pleasurable. He has worked on synthesising the conflicting parts of his personality and to be as whole and complete as is possible.

Transforming Interpersonal Loneliness

The means of transforming Interpersonal Loneliness focus more on ways of doing than of being. Loneliness is dissolved by doing, by acting, by being involved; it is practical and hands-on. The work has an external rather than an inner orientation.

Here are 8 practical solutions:

1. Befriending Schemes

Age UK has developed what are known as befriending services. The befriender is allocated a person to befriend and, according to the Age UK website, the befriender will provide conversation and companionship over a long period of time.

"Many local Age UKs provide befriending services, some by telephone and some where a volunteer visits the older person at their home. This vital service provides a link to the outside world and often acts as a gateway for other services and valuable support. Age UK also provides a telephone befriending service called *Call In Time* which consists of a regular daily or weekly phone call. The relationship is structured so that each befriender makes the call at a regular pre-agreed time. All befrienders are volunteers, who freely give up their time to help lonely older people."[56]

2. Volunteering

Becoming a volunteer may be challenging if you are feeling lonely. The small amount of effort required to start as a volunteer will be repaid abundantly by the opportunity to make new friends and to build a new social network as well as by knowing that you are being of service to others less fortunate than yourself.

3. Social Networks

There are very few examples of successful social networks which have been established specifically for the ageing. One of these is "Men in Sheds", run by Age UK in Cheshire; it is aimed, as the name suggests, at men and encourages them to meet once or twice a week to do woodwork and to socialise.

There may be something similar in your area, but if not, you could approach your local Age UK and discuss ways in which you could collaboratively start something.

---

[56] The Age UK website can be found at: www.ageuk.org.uk. A list of organisations, addresses, phone numbers and websites is given in Appendix F.

4. Technology

The best known examples of web-based social networks are Facebook, Twitter and Mumsnet, although none of these is specifically targeted at the ageing and, in my judgment, are no substitute for face-to-face interaction.

However, the Saga website[57] does have information of interest to older people and Saga Connections is an internet dating service for older people. Dating does not have to involve an intimate relationship and can be used as much for friendship as for romance!

Dr Meredith Belbin, who developed and very successfully marketed the Belbin Team Roles profiling system, has just launched a service for the over 50s known as "We Are Better Together"[58]. His unique profiling and matching system (which includes a phone interview with a facilitator) is the outcome of extensive research and a pilot scheme in Cambridgeshire. It offers the over 50s a number of options; sharing their home, sharing their interests, sharing holidays and, for those looking for closer relationships, the option of sharing their life.

5. Join In And Join Up

Every community, however small or however rural, has organisations or clubs which you can join.

Sandra lives in a village of around 800 people where there is a whole host of societies covering every imaginable activity - walking, ballet, flower arranging, handicrafts, lunch club, music appreciation, book club, choir, art, gardening, local

---

[57] The Saga website can be found at: www.saga.co.uk.
[58] The We Are Better Together website is at www.wearebettertogether.co.uk. The phone number is 0871 7810777 and they can be contacted between 9am and 5pm, Monday to Friday when "there will be real people answering the telephone; but there will be an answering machine at all other times. We do have to go home and sleep!" A list of organisations, addresses, phone numbers and websites is given in Appendix F.

history, folk dance, skittles, table tennis, football, ladies rounders and, yes, some of these do require a degree of mobility, but there is a pub, a church, and volunteers are always in demand for the community-run village shop. You may not be active or mobile, but the main entry requirement for most of these groups is turning up! You may no longer play football or cricket, Sandra plays neither, but she finds there are always opportunities to contribute in some way which will be appreciated.

You may be reading this and saying 'Well, that's all fine and dandy, but there's no theatre / macramé / politics / hang-gliding group where I live'. If you are right and this is so, then start one. Sandra organises one-off visits to concerts and the theatre, none of which have resulted in proposals of marriage, but she has got to know more people!

The actual activity is largely irrelevant, what is important is that you will meet people and you will make friends. As an Innate Loner, Sandra is still surprised when walking through her village how much of her time is spent talking to people she meets on the way – and most of them are people she has met through 'turning up' at these groups.

6. *Transform Your Relationships With Difficult People*

You may be one of those unusual people who gets on with everybody. If you are, then ask yourself if you're being completely honest with yourself – are you just avoiding people you don't like? Terry's strategy is to give people he doesn't like a wide berth, but occasionally he has to be in the company of people he is not keen on. These are typically people who have a different view of the world from him, holding opinions or having values diametrically opposed to his own, or whose demeanour and appearance he finds unsettling.

There is an explanation for this. It is understandable that those whose beliefs and values Terry does not share may cause him discomfort, but how about the others, the ones he dislikes on sight? Most likely is that they reflect parts of himself that he is not comfortable with. Terry finds he has a particularly strong reaction to people who are negative or judgmental. Why is this? Terry's conclusion is that in his misspent past he has done his share of homing-in on the negative, of criticising others, of looking for weakness in others and exploiting it.

If you are having a problem with someone, the exercise below will transform your experience. You may not end up being bosom buddies but you will get along better and will wonder whatever the fuss was about. There are three positions and seven steps.

Getting On With Difficult People

There are 3 positions:

① yourself

② the other person

③ the observer

There are 7 steps:

Step 1

① ——▶ ②

From position ① look at the other person ② and imagine or visualise this person being present. Out loud say what you think and feel about them. Really get fully into this. Do not hold back. You are on your own – you don't have to be polite!

Step out of position ① and dance a little jig to break your state.

Step 2

① ◀——②

Move into position ② looking at position ① which is you. Pretend to be the person in position ②, take on their

154

posture, their facial expression and bearing (it's OK, no-one is looking!), becoming as much like them as you possibly can. Speaking as if you truly are person ②, say out loud what you think and feel about the person in position ①. Go for it.

Step out of the position, dance a jig, and break state.

Step 3

From position ③, the observer position, look at positions ① and ② and say out loud what it is you observe. Be as objective as possible, resisting the temptation to be judgmental or critical.

Now list three resources, qualities or actions which you as the observer in position ③ thinks the person in position ① needs to improve the situation. Go through each of the three resources / qualities and remember a time when you had that quality, go back to that time and get a feel for what that memory was like. Repeat the process for the two other qualities.

Do not break state - no need for frenzied jigging!

Step 4

Move out of position ③ so you are standing outside of all the positions at ●

①   ②

                    ●

   ③

Take the three resources / qualities you uncovered in position ③ and transfer them over to position ①. You can do this by pretending to pick them up with your hands

155

and moving them to position ①. See them landing at position ①.

Step 5

① —→ ②

Standing in position ① receive the resources / qualities which have been transferred. Feel them coming in one by one and embedding themselves within you. Really feel this happening and notice when each one has arrived.

Step 6

① ◄—②

Move to position ②, the other person, and once again take on their posture, facial expression and bearing. Look at the person who has the new resources / qualities in position ① and say out loud how person ① seems to be now that they have these resources / qualities.

Step out of position ②, dance your dance again and break state.

Step 7

①—→ ②

Go back to position ① as yourself and say out loud how you are feeling now. You **will** notice a difference.

7. Develop Your Social Skills

Social skills are learned. You learned them from your parents, your teachers and your peers. If your parents were socially awkward, it is a reasonable bet that you are too.

When you meet people for the first time you have a very short period in which to get on their wavelength and build rapport with them. Rapport is the foundation of successful relationships and learning a skill which enables you to do this quickly will build your confidence in forming friendships.

156

A simple technique[59] will facilitate building rapport with other people. You will need to come to the encounter with the other person with an attitude of respect and a genuine wish to understand them and their reality.

Building Rapport

As a generalisation, people warm towards people who are similar to them and shy away from people who are different. The conclusion is that the more you are like the other person, the better they will respond to you. The technique of Matching and Mirroring will allow you to be similar to the other person without sacrificing any of your authenticity – you will be you and will remain you. What you are doing is to match the other person and to mirror aspects of them back to them.

Two tips:

[1] Avoid precisely replicating the movements, tone of voice or language of the other person - it will be noticed quickly and may be interpreted as taking-the-mickey. You are matching and mirroring, not copying;

[2] Avoid becoming so absorbed in the process that you stop listening to what they are saying – a rapid way to break rapport is to look as though you are not engaged!

You can match and mirror:

- Body – posture, movement, gestures, breathing, eye movements.

- Voice – pitch, speed, tone, volume.

- Language – the words and vocabulary they use.

- Values – where you have common values match and mirror their enthusiasm.

- Interests – reflect back your own enthusiasm where

---

[59] In NLP this technique is called 'Matching & Mirroring'

you have coincidental interests.

Whatever they do, you do the same ... but not so that they notice!

1. Take on the same body posture of the other.

Are they upright or leaning backwards or forwards? Notice their breathing – is it fast or slow, deep or shallow? Do they move around as they speak or are they still? Do they use hand gestures? If they are sitting, are their arms folded or loose in their lap, are their legs crossed, are their feet poised to spring or relaxed and apart? Do they hold unwavering eye contact?

Whatever they do, you do the same ... but not so that they notice!

2. Notice their voice.

Is the pitch high, low or somewhere in between? Do they speak fast or slow? Is the tone staccato or legato? Do they speak loud or soft?

Whatever they do, you do the same ... but not so that they notice!

3. Be sensitive to the words they use.

And be cautious and selective in what you match. Where possible use their words rather than yours - an exaggerated example is where you are speaking to an American. Resist the temptation to substitute 'boot' for 'trunk' or 'trousers' for 'pants'. By using the same words they use you are acknowledging the other person and the consequence of this is that they feel they have been listened to and heard.

Whatever they do, you do the same ... but not so that they notice!

4. Match and mirror their values while remaining authentic and congruent.

If you have mismatching values remain silent while appearing interested. If your values overlap you can show your enthusiasm with an appropriate level of nodding and positive interjections – 'Oh yes', 'Absolutely', 'I totally agree'!

Whatever they do, you do the same ... but not so that they notice!

5. You may have corresponding interests.

Mirror their enthusiasm and allow your face to show your own passion. If you have some opposing interests, it may be prudent to maintain rapport by appearing curious without being openly antagonistic! By being enquiring, it is possible to stay in rapport without sacrificing your own opinions and beliefs.

Whatever they do, you do the same ... but not so that they notice!

8. Leave Your Anxieties At Home

Even the most socially adept and confident can at times find meeting people brings up anxieties. Nervousness is a handicap on such occasions and you can use the visualisation technique below to dump your anxieties at the door, or leave them at home.

The Black Box[60]

Having identified what it is that is bothering you, sit quietly, close your eyes, take a deep breath and allow yourself to settle heavily into your chair as you breathe out slowly.

Imagine yourself sitting at a desk in front of a

---

[60] This technique was developed by John Syer and Christopher Connolly and is to be found in: Syer, J., and Connolly, C., *Sporting Body, Sporting Mind: An Athlete's Guide to Mental Training,* Simon & Schuster Ltd, 1987, pp 14-15

window. Look out and notice what you see, what the weather is like, what movement there may be. Then look down at the desk and notice a blank sheet of paper and a pen. Pick up the pen and write down a complete list of those distractions and concerns you identified. As you write, see the shape of your handwriting on the page, hear the point of your pen slide over the paper, feel the weight of your upper body on your arm. If you find it easier you can draw a picture to represent the distractions or your distracted mood.

When you have finished, see yourself put down the pen, fold up the piece of paper and turn around. You see a box behind you, somewhere within reach. It may be on a shelf or on the floor. Notice how large it is, what colour it is and whether it is in the light or the shadow. Open the lid. Then put the folded piece of paper inside the box, close the lid and turn back to the desk, settling back into your chair and once more looking out of the window.

Having done this, you can open your eyes.

Transforming Innate Loneliness

Feeling lonely is a state of mind; **your** state of mind. And you can change it. The approaches described below will make it possible for you to make the changes necessary. They are:

      A. Psychological Therapies.
      B. Destroying Limiting Beliefs.
      C. Reframing Your Inner Voice.
      D. Zapping Negative Thoughts.
      E. Visualisation of a Rich And Rewarding Social Life.
      F. Befriending Your Inner Buddy.

A. Psychological Therapies.

If you related to Ken's history described earlier in this chapter it may be that some form of therapy[61] would be advisable to break down the barriers which are keeping you isolated. If you came from a dysfunctional or chaotic family, you could benefit from a form of group or individual therapy known as Family Constellations which helps you to psychologically reconfigure your family in a way which is more orderly and better functioning. Do be aware though that this may only be the start and that the impact of this reconstruction can throw up a variety of issues with which you might need further support.

To find out more about Constellations, visit the website of the Centre For Systemic Constellations[62]. One of the leading Constellations practitioners in the UK is Judith Hemming and her website includes an excellent article about what happens in Constellations workshops[63].

The forming of satisfactory friendships and intimate relationships may be inhibited by what is known as Social Anxiety Disorder (abbreviated to SAD). Described as "a marked and persistent fear of negative evaluation in social or performance situations", SAD is most commonly treated by Cognitive Behavioural Therapy (CBT). The website of The British Association for Behavioural & Cognitive Psychotherapies (BABCP)[64] has a section describing what CBT is and where you can search for a CBT therapist.

Your issues may stem from factors which are more general and which may not have their origins in childhood. It

---

[61] A list of the different types of psychological therapies is to be found at Appendix E.
[62] www.centreforsystemicconstellations.com
[63] http://www.movingconstellations.com/media/pdf_media/wave-nov2005.pdf
[64] The website of The British Association for Behavioural & Cognitive Psychotherapies can be found at www.babcp.com. A list of organisations, addresses, phone numbers and websites is given in Appendix F.

may be that you do have some concerns which are interfering with your life today, or, you may just need someone to talk to with whom you can unburden yourself, and there is a wide variety of therapies from which you can choose. The British Association for Counselling & Psychotherapy (BACP)[65] website has an excellent section on Seeking A Therapist, which will tell you also what therapy is and what to expect. It has a list of therapists which you can search by postcode and, if you wish, by your reasons for seeking therapy and the type of approach you are looking for.

B. Destroying Limiting Beliefs

A limiting belief is one which holds you back and sucks the energy out of you. It is a belief which is not empowering.

Although you cannot see your limiting beliefs, they can have a powerful grip. For example, if, like Ken, you have the limiting belief that you are unlovable, then you will most likely avoid experiences involving other people and will miss out on the possibility of making new connections.

Most limiting beliefs are acquired during childhood, although this is not always the case. Whenever your limiting beliefs were formed, the pattern is the same: you drew a conclusion from one or more specific events and then constructed a false belief based on this conclusion.

Limiting beliefs can be challenged and changed. The exercise below specifically addresses limiting beliefs you may hold about loneliness, but it can be used to remove any limiting beliefs you may have in other areas of your life.

---

[65] The website of The British Association for Counselling & Psychotherapy can be found at www.bacp.co.uk. A list of organisations, addresses, phone numbers and websites is given in Appendix F.

Destroying Your Limiting Beliefs About Loneliness

Step 1: Identify Your Limiting Belief(s)

Limiting beliefs keep you stuck where you are and stop you moving forward and getting what you want. If, for example, you believe that nobody loves you, you will most likely avoid any social situation where there is the possibility of rejection, however remote.

The first step is to tease out the limiting beliefs you might hold about loneliness.

To do this, I invite you to look at what stops you having what it is you want. For example, you may want a rich, fulfilling social life.

There are 12 statements. To help you complete them I have given you some questions in the adjacent column to prompt you. In your Journal write the completed statement.

	Statement	Prompts To Help You Complete The Statement
1	If I get what I want then _____	*What might you lose? What might go wrong? What would you have to give up or change?*
2	I'll always have this problem because _____	*What can't you change that stops you from getting what you want?*
3	Getting what I want will make _____	*What problems would arise if you did get what you want?*
4	There is a part of me that does not want this goal because	*What are you avoiding? What are you afraid of?*

5	It is not possible for me to get what I want because	*What makes it impossible for you to get what you want?*
6	I am not capable of getting what I want because	*What are you incapable of doing that means you are not able to have what you want?*
7	causes things to stay the way they are now	*What is stopping you from making changes?*
8	Things will never get better because	*What will stop things getting better?*
9	The situation will never change because of	*What is stopping change? What hurdles are just too big for you to jump?*
10	I don't deserve to get what I want because	*What have you done that makes you unworthy or undeserving?*
11	Getting what I want would mean	*What would be the negative impact? What would be the impact on other people?*
12	It is wrong to want to be different because	*What makes you wanting what you want wrong or inappropriate?*

Look at your statements and pull out the belief that is embedded in what you have written.

For example, if for number 12 you have written "It is wrong to want to be different because I might disgrace myself", what is the belief that lies behind this? Is it that you have a belief that you might disgrace yourself. This is indeed a limiting belief and would hold you back from doing what you want.

When you have identified your limiting beliefs, write them in your Journal. For each one ask whether it is exactly right? Is there another form of words which would express the belief more accurately?

Step 2: Questions About Your Beliefs

So that you bring your limiting beliefs more fully into your conscious awareness, which will begin the process of transforming them, I would like you to answer some questions about each one and to write the answers in your Journal:

Have I always believed this?

Where did this belief come from?

Is the belief still valid today?

What evidence do I have to support this belief?

Who do I know who holds an opposite belief?

What evidence do I have that the belief is no longer true?

In what way is the belief absurd or ridiculous?

By answering these simple questions, you will begin to let some light and air into your belief; it will become less rigid and you may begin to see that it is invalid and perhaps ridiculous!

Step 3: Empowering Beliefs

Look at your list of limiting beliefs from Step 1 and search your mind for a belief or beliefs which would be more empowering and positive. Next to each of your limiting beliefs write an empowering belief.

If you are inspired you can write more empowering beliefs than you have limiting beliefs. For example:

Limiting belief = I might disgrace myself / Empowering belief = I respect myself

Limiting belief = I have no friends / Empowering belief = I have many close friends.

Limiting belief = Nobody loves me / Empowering belief = I am loved.

Empowering belief = I have a rich and rewarding social life.

Empowering belief = I enjoy meeting people.

Step 4: Checking Your New Beliefs Are Right For You

Close your eyes; take a few breaths in and out and let your body relax. Imagine yourself with one of your new beliefs. See yourself doing things differently. Visualise yourself with this new belief talking to and meeting other people in a different way. Notice how good this makes you feel. Observe the impact of your new belief on other people.

Ask yourself:

[1] Is this new belief right for me?

[2] Am I able to do what is necessary for it to be a reality?

[3] What will this new belief do for me? How will it be of benefit to me?

[4] What do I need to do to make this belief even better for me?

[5] How will I know when this belief is working for me?

What will be the evidence?

Repeat the process for all your new beliefs, one by one. If your answer to the questions is not positive or if this belief feels in some way not quite right, choose another from your list of empowering beliefs and repeat Step 4 until you are certain you have the right one(s).

C. Reframing Your Inner Voice

You may have an inner critical voice which is giving you messages which are keeping you lonely and isolated. Chances are that this voice came from a parent or authority figure who repeatedly criticised or belittled you. Continual derogatory comments - such as "Who's a little Show-Off", "Who do you think you are", "Whoever would want (to marry) you", "Look at the state of you" - will have chipped away at your self-confidence and self-esteem to the extent that you have difficulty forming meaningful, healthy relationships. You will have unconsciously internalised this voice so that every time you hear it you are reinforcing the thoughts, feelings and behaviours that go with it. It is not helpful.

Cynthia had an aunt who, she now realises, was sympathetic to her loneliness as an only child with alcoholic parents. This was not apparent to her at the time and she recalls how miserable she felt when her aunt would say "You're a lonely little girl" and would emphasize this by giving her books with titles like "Fun for One". Cynthia internalised this voice and many years later in her 50s would find herself thinking "I am lonely".

How did Cynthia work with her "I am lonely" inner voice? By reframing it using an adaptation of a process called "Six step reframing" developed by Richard Bandler and John Grinder.[66]

---

[66] Richard Bandler and John Grinder, *Frogs into Princes.* Moab, Utah: Real People Press, 1979

Reframing Your Inner Voice

Process	*Cynthia's Reframing*
Step 1: Critical Inner Voice	
Think of a time when your inner voice criticised you. Go back to that time in your imagination and listen to that voice. Notice how it sounds – the tone, speed, rhythm, volume and pitch of the voice.	*Her inner voice is telling her that she is lonely.*
Step 2: Positive Intention	
Ask your voice, "What is your positive intention?" Listen to what the voice has to say and repeat the question until you are comfortable with the response you get.	*At first, her voice gave her some intentions which were negative and she realises that this is her critical voice talking, so she repeats the question.*
	After a while her voice comes up with a positive intent which is "To keep you safe". This feels right for her.
Step 3: Acknowledge and Thank	
Acknowledge the voice for giving you this positive intention and agree with it.	*Cynthia says, "Thank you for telling me that your positive intention is to keep me safe, I agree with this."*

Step 4: Ask the voice to join in a search for alternatives

Ask the voice, "If there were additional ways to get this positive intention that were at least as good as, or even better than' what you are now doing, would you be interested in trying them out?"

Wait for a wholehearted Yes.

Step 5: Engage your creative part

Ask the creative part of you to generate an abundance of possible behaviours which would transform the critical voice.

The voice will choose three of them which it feels will work well for you and be better than your current behaviour.

Cynthia asked the voice and, to her surprise, quickly received an enthusiastic Yes!

Cynthia asked a creative part of her to come up with a lot of alternative behaviours to transform her loneliness. She wrote these down in her Journal and asked the voice to choose the three best. They were:

1. Go to a cookery class.

2. Take up ballroom dancing.

3. Invite someone to supper once a week.

She was aligned with these. They addressed

her loneliness without compromising her safety.

Step 6: Future Planning

Choose **one** of the three behaviours. Close your eyes, take a few breaths in and out and let your body relax. Imagine yourself carrying out this new activity to see how well it works. Notice how this makes you feel.

Repeat the process for the two other behaviours.

If any of them feels in some way not quite right, repeat step 5 to generate more options.

In your Journal write down these new behaviours and commit to carrying them out.

Cynthia imagined herself carrying out these new ways of being and behaving. She wrote them down in her Journal.

At the cookery class, Cynthia met a number of older single women like herself. At her suggestion, the Crumbling Cookies (as they call themselves) meet in one of their houses to try out the new recipes they have learned.

At the ballroom dancing she met Ted who had been recently widowed. The Crumbling Cookies tease her that she is being pursued for her Steak & Kidney Pudding!

D. Zapping Negative Thoughts

Negative thoughts will intrude periodically and do their best to demoralise you. As you anticipate turning up for your first game with the Bald Blokes' Bowling Club, or, you are walking to the

170

whist drive, tiny niggling doubts may creep into your mind. You can change this negative thinking by taking a few breaths and zapping the thoughts.

Changing Negative Thoughts to Positive

To change a negative thought into a positive one:

1. Visualize the two thoughts:

    a. The negative one.

    b. The positive one you want to replace the negative one.

2. Imagine the negative thought in your left hand.

3. Imagine the positive thought in your right hand and make this image as bright, clear and positive as you can.

4. Put your left hand in front of you and the right hand behind you.

5. To effect the change, move your left hand behind you and your right hand in front of you in a <u>very</u> fast movement. Repeat 10 times.

E. Visualisation of a rich and rewarding social life

Visualisation has the power to transform: to change anxiety into tranquillity, hopelessness into hope, and despair into delight. It can be used to overcome fear, to achieve goals, to build self-confidence and self-esteem. As with many of the skills set out in this book, it requires practice, but once embedded it is there as an ally for a lifetime.

Many of us think visually. If you think back to your last holiday, how do you remember it? In words? Sounds? As a sensation in your body? Or in pictures? One of Belinda's more memorable holidays was a trip to New York in the heat and humidity of an east coast August; when she thinks of it now, it is in a series of images: The subway, standing at the top of the

Empire State, a picnic in Central Park, walking round the site of the World Trade Centre, etc. This brings the holiday back to her in a very intense way. Not only can she see it, but she can feel the heat and smell the emanations of the subway; she can see, taste and smell the cocktails she and Basil had before they ate their 16oz steak and chips!

The step from thinking visually to visualisation is a small one. It formalises something you have been doing most of your life; a structure to which the power of visual thinking can be attached and a framework to customise, adapt and modify the visual material to produce a desired outcome.

Visualisation is effective because, although it is a very sophisticated mechanism, the central nervous system does not differentiate between real and imagined events. Have you ever woken from a nightmare in a panic with your heart pounding believing that you really had been chased down the street by a tiger? You have been having a dream, but your nervous system has been behaving <u>as though it were real</u>. My experience is that these really vivid nightmares or dreams can take a while to recover from. This is because they have impressed themselves upon both your visual and your muscle memory – the mental images have primed the body for physical action.

Some people find visualisation easy; it comes naturally to them. They close their eyes and images flood into their mind. For others it is more difficult. However, you do process a lot of information visually. For example, how do you recognise your spouse across a crowded room? By comparing the person you see at the other end of the room with the visual memory you have of him/her. But if you do have difficulty visualising, pretend that you can and that will remove the block.

In the exercise below, you are going to visualise a rich and rewarding social life. This is your opportunity to create the best social life for yourself. It will be and will become your social life – not someone else's and not a carbon copy of something you have seen on TV.

This exercise requires some preparation and you should allow plenty of time to do the visualisation itself.

Visualising A Rich And Rewarding Social Life

Step 1: Preparation

In your Journal write down or draw the ingredients of a social life which you would find rich and rewarding. This may be regular coffee dates with a couple of friends; it may be a non-stop merry-go-round of dinners, dances, parties, celebrations. Be unconstrained and keep it realistic.

Continue to add things to the list. Do not limit yourself.

Once you have done this (for now) put the list to one side and go and do something else. Other thoughts and ideas will occur to you, most likely at unexpected times. Go back to the list and write them down.

Step 2: Warm Up 1

As with any exercise it is sensible to warm up first rather than dive straight in. To get your visual muscles flexed, go through the following.

• Close your eyes. Sit with your feet on the floor with your hands resting loosely in your lap.

• Breathe out and then IN to the count of 4, HOLD for the count of 2, breathe out to the count of 6, pause for the count of 2 and repeat the cycle five times. Make sure that you do not exaggerate your breathing and that the out-breath is longer and slower than the in-breath.

• Consciously relax. Check the areas of tension in your body and allow the tension to flow away through your fingers and toes.

• Imagine each of the following in turn:

▪ SEE: the sun rising out of the sea; the front door of

the last house you lived in.

- HEAR: a nail being hammered into a piece of wood; a dog barking in the distance.

- FEEL: your hands being warmed in front of a log fire; snow falling on your face.

- SMELL: freshly baked bread; leather.

- TASTE: the segment of an orange; a sip of coffee.

Notice which of these you found easy and which more difficult. If you found it more difficult to see, do not be put off. Try again, allowing random images to come into your head, and rather than aiming to 'see' an image, 'think' about it instead.

In the next stage of the Warm Up, you will practise first the skill of visualising externally, seeing yourself as if you are in a film being shown on a cinema screen, and then of visualising internally, floating into your own body in the film on the cinema screen. Viewing the action from inside your own body intensifies the experience and integrates it more fully into your body, mind and emotions.

Step 3: Warm Up 2

- Close your eyes.

- Begin with breathing and relaxation (as in Step 2).

- Imagine yourself sitting in a cinema.

- See yourself on the screen eating an apple.

- Slowly zoom in and make the image brighter, sharper, louder, clearer.

- Turn the image into black and white; and then back into colour.

- Slowly zoom out and make the image more distant,

174

duller, softer, less focussed, quieter.

• Imagine floating up out of your seat in the cinema and up into the image on the screen and into your own body. Seeing what you see, hearing what you hear, feeling what you feel from inside your body. Open your eyes.

Step 4: Ground Rules

• Always, always begin with breathing and relaxation, using the now familiar pattern at the beginning of Step 2.

• Be positive: be sure to visualise what you want, <u>not</u> what you are aiming to get away from (e.g. "I want 3 close friends" <u>not</u> "I don't want to be lonely anymore").

• Be specific: imagine as much detail as you can: where you are, what you are wearing, what you are seeing, hearing and feeling.

• See, hear and feel perfection: don't be satisfied with second best, imagine everything exactly as you want it to be.

• Use all of your senses: sound, sight, bodily sensations, smell, taste, emotions.

• Ideally, visualise externally (seeing yourself on the cinema screen) until you have the images which are 'right', and then visualise internally (from inside your own body).

Step 5: Creating Your Rich, Rewarding Social Life

Re-read the notes you made in your Journal in Step 1 to refresh your memory of the social life you want.

• Close your eyes; breathe and relax.

• See yourself in a film on the cinema screen living your rich and rewarding social life. Create as much detail as possible. Adjust the image so that it is brighter, sharper, louder, clearer, closer.

- See everything as being perfect. Notice what you can see, hear and feel as you observe yourself. What are you wearing? What are you doing? What are you saying? How are you standing? What is the expression on your face?

- When this image is good enough, take a deep breath and watch the scene from somewhere else – nearer / farther, front / sideways / behind, above / below, etc.

- Only when this image is perfect in every detail and you are completely happy with the social life you have created for yourself, float up out of your cinema seat and step inside the image of yourself in the film on the screen. Be aware of being **fully present inside** your body.

- Relive the experience you created when you were sitting in the cinema. This time be right in it. You are no longer an observer; you are you. Enjoy the experience.

- If you are not fully satisfied with the visualisation and you feel it could be improved or there are details missing, go back and see yourself on the cinema screen until you *are* satisfied and then float back into your own body again.

- Repeat the internal visualisation at least five times to imprint it on your unconscious mind. It will become easier the more you do it.

F. Befriending Your Inner Buddy

One of the features of childhood development is the imaginary friend. Research suggests that the imaginary friend is an expression of a child's anxieties, fears and hopes and this is evident if you have ever heard a child having a conversation with their friend. Some children become so engrossed in this fantasy that they see their friend as a physical entity indistinguishable from a real person; for others, the friend exists only in their imagination or is felt as a presence. While common in children, imaginary friends are regarded as abnormal in adults.

The friend I have in mind for you is an Inner Buddy. Inner Buddies are attractive to the Innate Loner, being an opportunity to have a constant, unchanging companion who will never humiliate or abandon you. Some Innate Loners have an intense longing for something which they find hard to articulate that will fill their inner meaninglessness and isolation. Roberto Assagioli, who has a better informed and more lucid psychological vocabulary than an Innate Loner, describes this feeling as "Divine Homesickness", that feeling of existential emptiness or intense loneliness accompanied by a desire for something which is other and beyond.

Zak is a successful and wealthy internet entrepreneur in his early 50s; while messing around on his computer he developed a new online game which he has marketed globally. Living in a large house in West London which he shares with his girlfriend, he drives an electric car in town and has a Range Rover for weekends at his house in the country. He appears regularly on TV and is regarded by the media as a 'celebrity'. Nevertheless he feels very alone and misunderstood. He struggles to rationalise the fact that he has 'everything' with the feeling that there is a hole in his life, that something, though he cannot articulate what, is missing. The chances are that he is suffering from Divine Homesickness, the lack of a connection with something greater than and beyond himself.

Let me introduce you to your Inner Buddy, your best friend, who is 'other and beyond'. This visualisation is transformational – your Inner Buddy will melt your loneliness and become a strong unifying centre around which the rest of your personality will cluster.

Befriending Your Inner Buddy

This approach is similar to the Meeting with your Inner Guide described above in Chapter 13. This time, I want you to do some preparation.

Step 1: Preparation

With your Journal to hand, spend time thinking about what sort of person would be your ideal friend. Focus on the inner aspects of your ideal Inner Buddy, letting go of any concerns about gender, appearance, social background, status, clothes, etc. Home in on the qualities they would have, the values and beliefs they would hold, the skills and capabilities they would possess and write these down.

Once you have done this (for now) put the list to one side and go and do something else. Other thoughts and ideas will occur to you, most likely at unexpected times. Go back to the list and write them down.

Step 2: Befriending Your Buddy

•   Make yourself comfortable and ensure you are warm. Close your eyes, breathe and relax.

•   Visualise yourself going to a peaceful place such as a meadow. Visualise this place as fully as you can - seeing what you see, hearing what you hear and feeling what you feel. Take time to see the grass and the flowers, to hear the birds and the sounds of nature, to feel calm and serene.

•   Look around and you see a mountain. You decide to climb the mountain.

•   Begin your journey by entering a forest. Smell the scent of the pine trees, and sense the cool, dark, atmosphere.

•   Leave the forest, going out into warmth and sunlight again, and begin your ascent of the mountain. Feel the energy required to walk uphill, and notice the ease with which you are able to do this.

•   Approaching the top of the mountain notice how it is

rocky and that the ascent is becoming harder. The air is fresher and there is complete silence.

- At the top of the mountain you go into cloud and you are enveloped in mist.

- Suddenly the mist clears and you can see the blue sky, everything is brighter, and the final ascent is easier.

- Once at the very top, you are on a vast plateau, the silence is total, the sky is the very deepest blue.

- Far off you see someone. It is your Inner Buddy. This wonderful person will be your constant and unchanging companion for life and through all eternity. This person will love you unconditionally, accepting all of you unquestioningly and uncritically – your faults, your wrongdoings, your loneliness, your guilt and your shame. It is a profound moment.

- Walk towards each other slowly. Feel yourself filling up with an intense radiant love for this person.

- Face each other, look into your Buddy's eyes and say "I love you". Appreciate their inner and outer beauty.

- Listen as your Inner Buddy replies "I love you". Feel love entering your body and filling your heart. You are overflowing with love and gratitude.

- Take your Inner Buddy's hand and say "We are together forever". Together, and hand in hand, begin slowly to descend the mountain, pass through the forest and return to the meadow.

- Open your eyes and return to normal waking consciousness.

I have guided clients through this Psychosynthesis visualisation and it is always an extremely moving experience for me as I lead them up the mountain and for them as they meet their Inner Buddy (or soul). I have never come to the end of this exercise (such a mundane word to describe something so intense) with dry eyes.

This is the true delight and the great gift of Psychosynthesis - that while our feet may be stuck in the mud, we can lift up our eyes and see the sun rising over distant hills.

Ageing Amazingly

15.
The Hero Returns

The Hero's Journey is a mythological story at the end of which the Hero returns to the world, to the old familiar places, but not to the old familiar ways. Although the world may look pretty much the same and he may not look radically different on the outside, the Hero begins to notice changes in his inner world. Perhaps he does not react to stimuli in the same way? Maybe he feels calmer? More at ease with himself? Conceivably his thoughts and feelings may be more positive? Possibly his outlook may be brighter?

So it can and will be for you. You have chosen through the course of this book to work on growing your Inner You by building the four cornerstones of Amazing Ageing - making choices, letting go of the past, accepting things just as they are, and developing gratitude. You have constructed the six pillars of Amazing Ageing by being positive, being realistic, taking action, being flexible, living your life without the restriction of outdated rules, and being resilient.

You may have taken enormous leaps forward or you may have shuffled no more than a few steps, it matters not. What does matter is that you have made a careful and conscious choice to set out on the journey *and* in taking one or more steps you have set up a process which can bring you only benefits.

You have taken some steps and maybe want to take some more. This final chapter will enable you to create a bright future for yourself, help you review the journey you have taken, and, finally, encourage you to open to endless possibility.

1. A Bright Future

Just imagine what your life might become if the four cornerstones and the six pillars were fully integrated into your everyday living. At the centre of your universe is You, surrounded by all the attributes of Amazing Ageing:

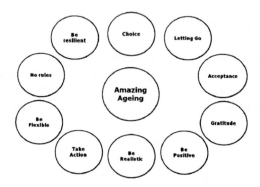

Your bright future will be one in which the life that lies ahead of you is so clearly imagined and of such power that it has a forceful impact on you in the present. Many musicians have a distinct idea of what it is they want to achieve; executing a particularly demanding passage flawlessly and gracefully or receiving the applause of the audience at the end of their performance. If you were to ask them about this 'distinct idea' they would be able to describe it colourfully and in detail. It is so strong for them that it is as if it actually exists. In fact, it is not so much an idea, more a representation of reality.

Your Bright Future

- Find somewhere that you can be comfortable and undisturbed. Relax by breathing in to the count of 4 and slowly to the count of 6.

- Look at the image above and become aware that these are the factors - ten of them - which will ensure that your own ageing is amazing.

- Allow the centre of the image to fade and replace it with a positive, happy picture of you. It may be a picture of your face, or a full head-to-toe body shot. Whichever you choose, be sure that it is you... and that it is upbeat and cheerful.

- Now close your eyes, but retain the image of you

surrounded by the ten attributes of Amazing Ageing.

- Bring the first of the four cornerstones - Choice - into the foreground by making it more prominent than the others. See it shining and shimmering in the same way that the sun shines on water. And now imagine a powerful current of energy flowing from that particular cornerstone into the My Amazing Ageing circle in the centre. Increase the power of the current... and then increase it some more. Feel the intense energy of the power of Choice flowing into you and becoming part of you.

- Allow Choice to move into the background and take its place with the ten other attributes.

- Repeat the process for the other cornerstones and pillars. If you need to remind yourself which one comes next, partially open your eyes so you can see which one it is.

- For each one, the process is:

  - Bring it into the foreground and see it shining and shimmering.

  - Imagine a powerful current flowing from it to the My Amazing Ageing circle in the centre. Increase the power of the current ... increase it even more.

  - Feel the energy flowing into you and becoming part of you.

  - Allow it to recede into the background.

- When you have brought each of the four cornerstones and six pillars into the foreground and have connected to the energy and power of each one, imagine yourself in the middle of this circle absorbing the powerful currents from all ten of them.

- You may find it helpful to imagine you are like a battery and see the level of energy within you rising, up and up.

- When you are fully (re)charged, gently open your eyes and return to the room.

- Now slowly say the following in a strong voice, repeating each line three times:

    - I carefully and consciously make choices which are right for me.

    - I let go of the past.

    - I accept things exactly as they are.

    - I am grateful for everything that happens to me.

    - I am positive.

    - I am realistic.

    - I take action.

    - I am flexible.

    - I am free from rules.

    - I am resilient.

- In your Journal, record your thoughts and feelings about this exercise. What did you notice? What did you learn? Were there any of the ten attributes which were more difficult in some way? Or easier?

2. Review

Let us go back to the starting point of the journey and explore, once again, Where You Are Now. This time, you will look at where you are now through fresh eyes; not only will the river have flowed on, but you will be stepping into it at a different point.

Where Are You Now?

- Take some crayons or coloured felt tip pens and some paper (or you can use a page of your Journal - if you have any pages left!)

- Sit in a comfortable chair and close your eyes.

- Allow your mind to focus softly on where you are in your life and ask yourself 'What is my life like now?'

- Now let your hand draw. Observe with detached curiosity the picture which emerges. Try and avoid judgement - it does not have to be perfect!

- Draw whatever comes. It may be an obvious representation of something or it may be formless, shapeless and fuzzy. Just let your hand (not your head) guide you.

- When you have finished, stand up and dance a little jig. Take a few deep breaths.

- Now look at what you have drawn. What is it saying to you? What feelings does it bring up? Do you feel happy or sad, calm or angry? Is it personal or impersonal? Warm or cold? Is there movement in your drawing or is it static - and what might this mean?

- Look at it from another angle - turn it sideways or the wrong way up - and ask yourself the same questions.

- Take time to reflect on what this drawing has to say to you about your life and where you are right now.

- In your Journal, record your reflections. As you write you may find that other things bubble up. Write them down.

- Take some more time for reflection, but this time focus on what has changed since you did this exercise the first time round (see Chapter 2). Ask yourself:

  - In what ways am I different? Home in on ways in which your thinking, your feelings and behaviour have changed. Are you making conscious choices? Are you less attached to old ways of thinking, feeling and being? Are you more accepting of how things are? More grateful? More positive? More realistic?

- In what ways are you the same? Consider this to be an audit of where work is still in progress or where work remains to be undertaken.

- You may want to look at some grey areas where you are uncertain about whether or not there has been change, and to monitor these in the future to check whether there has been movement or stagnation.

- In your Journal, record the changes you have noticed in yourself and write a short sentence of gratitude: "I am grateful that I am now ......"

- Record the audit of where work is still to be done. Aim to do this without any judgement in either the words you write on the page or in your thoughts as you write them; it is preferable that you take the position of the observer, noticing but not passing judgement.

- Finally, make a note of the fuzzy areas you want to keep an eye on.

You should now be clear what your next steps will be. You know what work is still to be done and what aspects of Amazing Ageing you need to keep an eye on.

3. Opening To Endless Possibility

I began this book by saying that the 'inner you' is the only part of you where growth can occur. It is appropriate to end with an exercise which affirms growth and encourages you to be open to what your life may be.

The Rose[67]

- Sit in a comfortable chair and close your eyes.

---

[67] From: Ferrucci, Piero. *What We May Be.* Turnstone. 1982. Pp 132-3

- Imagine a rosebush: roots, stem, leaves and, on top, a rosebud. The rosebud is closed, and enveloped by its green sepals. Take your time in visualising all the details clearly.

- Now imagine that the sepals start to open, turn back, and reveal the petals inside - tender, delicate, still closed.

- Now the petals themselves slowly begin to open. As they do so, you become aware of a blossoming also occurring in the depths of your being. You feel that something in you is opening and coming to light.

- As you keep visualising the rose, you feel that its rhythm is your rhythm, its opening is your opening. You keep watching the rose as it opens up to the light and the air, as it reveals itself in all its beauty.

- You smell its perfume and absorb it into your being.

- Now gaze into the very centre of the rose, where its life is at its most intense. Let an image emerge from there. This image will represent what is most beautiful, most meaningful, most creative that wants to come to light in your life right now. It can be an image of absolutely anything. Just let it emerge spontaneously without forcing or thinking.

- Now stay with this image for some time, and absorb its quality.

- The image may have a message for you - a verbal or non-verbal message. Be receptive to it.

Appendices

A.
Your Unconscious Mind

Although philosophers and mystics have known for centuries of the link between mind and body, it is only in recent times that scientists have established an irrefutable connection between the two. Without going into the science, it is sufficient to know that **what we think effects what we feel which effects how we behave**. You can easily test this for yourself by deliberately and consciously bringing to mind pleasant thoughts and notice how this makes you feel and what impact it has on your body. Now think gloomy thoughts. Do you notice the difference?

Thinking, feeling and behaviour are a loop or a system.

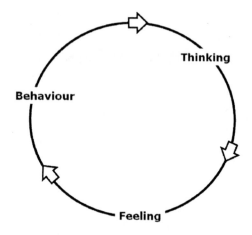

Like any system, a change in any one part of the system has an inevitable effect on the other two parts; if you change your thinking, then your feelings and your behaviour will change, etc.

The thinking part of the system, the mind, has two parts: the conscious and the unconscious mind. Our unconscious mind, by definition, is the part of us which contains everything of which we are not conscious. The unconscious mind is where change takes place, the conscious mind is where we become aware of the change, and the consequent behaviour is how we know that change has happened.

What you are thinking and what you are feeling at this present moment is taking place in your conscious mind, but these thoughts and feelings are the result of a process of which you are probably not conscious. You think you will go and make a cup of tea (conscious), an action which may be prompted by any one of a number of unconscious motivations - thirst, a desire for comfort / warmth / nourishment, or an antidote to fatigue.

The unconscious mind has a number of functions:
- It controls bodily processes (breathing, heartbeat, blood circulation, hunger, thirst);
- It is the source of dreams, creative ideas, intuition;
- It is the locus of memory;
- It is the place where we retain our:
  - Learned skills (how to turn on a tap);
  - Instincts (self-preservation, sexual desires);
  - Motivations (falling in love);
  - Emotions (joy, sadness, anger, compassion);
- … and it is a compelling driver of behaviour.

It is largely thanks to Freud that the unconscious has got a bad name for itself as the repository of base instincts and socially unacceptable desires. Indeed, these darker aspects may well be present in the unconscious, but it is more than that. It has light as well as shadow; it contains your potential, what you may become, and it has the positive function of keeping you alive by regulating bodily processes. Although the unconscious mind may harbour murderous thoughts about parents and unwanted sexual urges, it also ensures that you have sufficient oxygen, pump blood round your body as required, do not stick your hand in a fire and that you meet and mate, nourish and nurture. You cannot control these unconscious processes but you can influence them to work in your favour.

III

The unconscious mind is very literal and never lies. Because it is literal it is essential that you focus on and are very specific about what you want rather than what you don't want. All of the exercises and techniques in this book focus on the positive, on what you do want, and have a 'towards' rather than an 'away from' orientation. If you tell your unconscious mind you want to lose weight, my hunch is that it will focus on loss and weight; on the other hand if you say you want to have a 28" waist or to be healthy it will direct its attention toward that. Likewise, if you say you want to stop smoking, what will it latch on to? Yes, stopping and smoking.

Because it is literal, your unconscious mind will take the messages you give it and, if asked to, will carry them out to the letter. Although it is very powerful, it is limited by its inability to question or interpret. It does not engage in the sort of dialogue which King Midas might have found of value - "When you said you wanted everything you touch to turn to gold, did you really mean that to include your food and drink?"

B.
Psychosynthesis

Psychosynthesis has been described as being the world's best kept secret. And so it is!

Roberto Assagioli, the founding father of Psychosynthesis, was an Italian psychiatrist and one of the first two or three Italians to pioneer psychoanalysis in Italy. Soon after qualifying as a psychoanalyst, he became one of its critics, believing that psychoanalysis was only partial, neglecting the exploration of what Maslow would call "the farther reaches of human nature." In an interview with Sam Keen in *Psychology Today* in December 1974[68], Assagioli vividly describes the difference between Psychoanalysis and Psychosynthesis:

> 'In one of his letters Freud said, "I am interested only in the basement of the human being." Psychosynthesis is interested in the whole building. We try to build an elevator which will allow a person access to every level of his personality. After all, a building with only a basement is very limited. We want to open up the terrace where you can sun-bathe or look at the stars. Our concern is the synthesis of all areas of the personality. That means Psychosynthesis is holistic, global and inclusive. It is not against psychoanalysis or even behaviour modification but it insists that the needs for meaning, for higher values, for a spiritual life, are as real as biological or social needs.'

In opening up the terrace, Assagioli was referring to the higher potential contained within a human being. In the same way that the discarded junk of childhood in the basement can disturb our psychological wellbeing today, so too, denial or repression of higher potential can be psychologically disruptive.

---

[68] Keen, S. *The Golden Mean of Roberto Assagioli*. Psychology Today. December 1974

Freud was concerned more with the lower unconscious, once comparing the human mind to the city of Rome. The history of Rome goes downwards with a modern building built on top of a renaissance one, below which is a medieval one and finally a building of ancient Rome itself; so with the mind, behind the facade lie the remains of former times and earlier memories. Assagioli's model includes, as does Freud's, a lower unconscious, but importantly and distinctively includes also the dimension of a superconscious, that part of us which contains our highest potential – the Self, the domain of values and peak experiences. Psychosynthesis does not focus solely on the past hidden in the rubbish bins concealed deep in the bushes, but includes the future, our potential, which can be manifest in a way which brings purpose and meaning to life. This is the true joy of Psychosynthesis, the process of uncovering the murky contents of the unconscious is done in the context of the unfolding splendour of being human. There is a drive towards unity and union, harmony, oneness and wholeness. It is about who we are and what we may be.

Assagioli described Psychosynthesis therapy as being like rebuilding the terminus while keeping the trains running (while structural change takes place, the daily comings and goings continue). As a therapy it is both gentle and challenging, it is about unfolding rather than stripping back and stripping bare. Among the techniques are guided visualisation, free drawing, symbols, ideal models, inner dialogue, working with subpersonalities, writing a psychological Journal... and many others!

C.
Neuro Linguistic Programming (NLP)

Neuro-Linguistic Programming is a system of communication which includes *neurology, language* and *programming*. The neurological system controls how the body functions; language, how we communicate with others; programming with the ways in which we process information and construct meaning. As a whole it describes the relationship between mind (neuro) and language (linguistic) and how together they affect our body and behaviour (programming).

NLP was developed in California in the 1970s by Richard Bandler and John Grinder who wished to understand and model human excellence. They began by studying therapeutic excellence, in particular the work of Fritz Perls, Virginia Satir and Milton Erickson. They did not aim to construct elegant theories but to comprehend what really worked and what helped clients to make change in their lives. From this they discovered patterns of thought and behaviour which enabled them to create potent techniques which could be used to facilitate change in people's lives.

NLP is very practical and hands-on. The 'problem' is identified, the technique is applied, the change is tested to ensure it is robust and reliable. Job done!

NLP is very powerful. In my own area of expertise as a practitioner it has helped people to permanently overcome devastating stage fright and performance anxiety in the space of a single one hour session. Clients are grateful and amazed. Grateful that it works and amazed that it is so simple and involves so little input from the client.

This email from a rock musician is testimony to the effectiveness and simplicity of NLP:

"I had a gig last night, one that I would generally be pretty nervous beforehand. For a couple of days before the gig I regularly visualised myself playing a perfect performance and people coming up to me and saying they loved my playing. I got to the gig and did the breathing exercise as well as imagined a circle around my drums. Just before the gig I anchored in the circle of excellence...and RESULT! Probably the best gig I have played in a very long time! I was relaxed, positive and passionate! Everything we talked about happened and I had many people complimenting me afterwards."

D.
The Hero's Journey

The Hero's Journey comes from *A Hero With A Thousand* Faces by Joseph Campbell in which "A hero ventures forth from the world of common day into a region of supernatural wonder: fabulous forces are there encountered and a decisive victory is won: the hero comes back from this mysterious adventure with the power to bestow boons on his fellow man." [69]

There are 12 stages to the story[70] :

1. THE ORDINARY WORLD. The hero, uneasy, uncomfortable or unaware, is introduced sympathetically so the audience can identify with the situation or dilemma. The hero is shown against a background of environment, heredity, and personal history. Some kind of polarity in the hero's life is pulling in different directions and causing stress.

2. THE CALL TO ADVENTURE. Something shakes up the situation, either from external pressures or from something rising up from deep within, so the hero must face the beginnings of change.

3. REFUSAL OF THE CALL. The hero feels the fear of the unknown and tries to turn away from the adventure, however briefly. Alternately, another character may express the uncertainty and danger ahead.

4. MEETING WITH THE MENTOR. The hero comes across a seasoned traveller of the worlds who gives him or her training, equipment, or advice that will help on the journey. Or the hero reaches within to a source of courage and wisdom.

---

[69] Campbell, Joseph. The Hero with a Thousand Faces. Princeton: Princeton University Press, 1949. p.23.
[70] This summary is taken from www.thewritersjourney.com/hero's_journey.htm

5. CROSSING THE THRESHOLD. At the end of Act One, the hero commits to leaving the Ordinary World and entering a new region or condition with unfamiliar rules and values.

6. TESTS, ALLIES AND ENEMIES. The hero is tested and sorts out allegiances in the Special World.

7. APPROACH. The hero and newfound allies prepare for the major challenge in the Special world.

8. THE ORDEAL. Near the middle of the story, the hero enters a central space in the Special World and confronts death or faces his or her greatest fear. Out of the moment of death comes a new life.

9. THE REWARD. The hero takes possession of the treasure won by facing death. There may be celebration, but there is also danger of losing the treasure again.

10. THE ROAD BACK. About three-fourths of the way through the story, the hero is driven to complete the adventure, leaving the Special World to be sure the treasure is brought home. Often a chase scene signals the urgency and danger of the mission.

11. THE RESURRECTION. At the climax, the hero is severely tested once more on the threshold of home. He or she is purified by a last sacrifice, another moment of death and rebirth, but on a higher and more complete level. By the hero's action, the polarities that were in conflict at the beginning are finally resolved.

12. RETURN WITH THE ELIXIR. The hero returns home or continues the journey, bearing some element of the treasure that has the power to transform the world as the hero has been transformed.

E.

Types of Psychological Therapy

There is a wide variety of psychological therapies and the information below guides you through some of the most common.

Most of the ones listed[71]are what is known as talking therapies (the exception is the Emotional Freedom Technique) – that is you talk through your concerns with a qualified counsellor or psychotherapist. There is no clear definition of the difference between counselling and psychotherapy, although the UK Council for Psychotherapy regards psychotherapy as being more in-depth. Some therapies may be short term (typically 6 sessions) or long term (where sessions take place regularly over a period, sometimes of years).

Much research has shown that the type of therapy you choose is less important than the relationship which builds between you and the therapist.

Type of Therapy	Approach
Cognitive Behavioural Therapy (CBT)	Cognitive Behavioural Therapy uses a practical approach in which the therapist helps the client understand the relationship between beliefs, feelings, and thoughts and the effect these have on behaviour patterns and actions. The client learns that his or her perception will directly affect his or her reaction to certain conditions and circumstances and that this thought process is at the root of behaviour.
Emotional Freedom	Emotional Freedom Technique (EFT) is a

---

[71] I am grateful to the goodtherapy.org website which has a comprehensive list of the many types of therapy available and which provides the detailed description of each of the types given here: http://www.goodtherapy.org/types-of-therapy.html

Technique (EFT)	revolutionary treatment method that offers healing from physical and emotional pain and disease. Without the use of needles, this form of acupuncture uses the fingertips to stimulate energy points on the body. Developed by Gary Craig, this is an easily mastered technique that can be performed virtually anywhere. This treatment sprang from the Emotional Freedom Technique Discovery Statement that says, "The cause of all negative emotions is a disruption in the body's energy system."
Existential Psychotherapy	This unique style of therapy puts emphasis on the human condition as a whole. Existential Psychotherapy uses a positive approach that applauds human capacities while simultaneously maintaining a genuine perception of the limitations of the human being, spirit, and mind.
Family Constellations	Family Constellations is an approach for revealing the hidden dynamics in a family so that they can be worked with and healed. Developed by Bert Hellinger, Family Constellation technique involves family representation through the use of others. People are strategically positioned into family roles, including (sometimes) a person in place of the client, in order to bring the family dynamic to fruition. Through non-verbal communication, each member is engaged in a form of cohesive and independent communication that serves to represent the true nature of the family. The representatives are instructed by a facilitator to act on the emotions, including fears and wants, of each person involved. By doing this, light is shed on the dysfunctional aspects of the family unit. In a startlingly real way, the family dynamic is accurately depicted

and is oftentimes recognized by the members for the first time. Each person is intrinsically linked by what is referred to as a morphongenic field. This sense of connectedness is felt telepathically and is acutely present in family situations.

Gestalt Therapy

Gestalt Therapy focuses on here-and-now experience and personal responsibility. It was developed by Fritz Perls, Laura Perls, and Paul Goodman. The objective, in addition to overcoming symptoms, is to become more alive, creative, and free from the blocks of unfinished issues which may diminish optimum satisfaction, fulfilment, and growth.

Mindfulness Based Cognitive Therapy

Mindfulness Based Cognitive Therapy was derived from the original program created by Jon Kabat-Zinn, which is known as Mindfulness-based Stress Reduction (MBSR). This form of therapy has been shown to be extremely effective at liberating and empowering clients with various medical ailments, including hypertension, chronic pain, and cancer. In addition, this method works equally as well to relieve the symptoms of various psychological issues including anxiety and panic. The original platform was designed to address the needs of people who suffered from multiple events of depression.

Person Centred

Person Centred Therapy was developed by Carl Rogers. This type of therapy diverged from the traditional views of the therapist as an expert and moved instead toward a non-directive approach that embodied the theory of actualizing tendency. The theory of actualizing tendency says humans have the potential to discover the realization of their own personal abilities. The foundation of this method of therapy is derived from the belief that every human being strives to find their own fulfilment and the fulfilment of his or her own potential. Carl R. Rogers stated that, "Individuals have within themselves vast resources for self-understanding and for altering their self-concepts, basic attitudes, and self-directed behaviour; these resources can be tapped if a definable climate of facilitative psychological attitudes can be provided" (from Carl R. Rogers. *Way of Being*. Boston: Houghton Mifflin, 1980, p.115-117).

Psychodynamic Psychotherapy

Psychodynamic and insight therapies aim to help clients become aware of and experience their vulnerable feelings which have been pushed out of conscious awareness. The Psychodynamic approach states that everyone has an unconscious which holds and harbours painful and vulnerable feelings which are too difficult for the person to be consciously aware of. In order to keep painful feelings, memories, and experiences in the unconscious, people tend to develop defence mechanisms, such as denial, repression, rationalization, and others. According to Psychodynamic theory, these defences cause more harm than good and that once the vulnerable or painful feelings are processed the defence mechanisms reduce or resolve.

Psychoanalysis

Developed by Sigmund Freud, Modern Psychoanalysis is a dichotomy in psychology as it has been revered and refuted by the general public throughout the years. The success of this therapy, particularly in European countries, has served to sever it from its true roots. Psychoanalysis has been used in sociology, religion, literature, and even in mythology and through these mediums gained momentum and recognition with the general population. However, its therapeutic and clinical purposes were overshadowed by its cultural acceptance. Seen as one of the most influential theories in history, Psychoanalysis appeared in our culture as a revolutionary and innovative model of construction that dared to oppose and challenge existing formulations and morals. The debate continues to this day as to whether this pervading clinical method of therapy has any validity in modern behavioural medicine or if it merely represents a meandering and colourfully narrative description of Freud's own distorted perceptions and beliefs.

Psychosynthesis

In an attempt to broaden the basis of Freud's "talking cure," psychiatrist Roberto Assagioli developed Psychosynthesis by integrating imagination, will, and intuition into the traditional therapy. He drew from a person's own human capacities, including aspirations, spirit, and the centre or Self. Psychosynthesis has many practical applications and is often used in education, business, psychology, and spirituality. The primary goal of Psychosynthesis is to increase our sense of centre and create balance in our lives by utilising our free will and personal internal resources. This multi-dimensional form of therapy encourages clients to unify and embrace differences in others and promotes community responsibility and respect. Clients are instructed to discover oppositions within themselves and to use their higher wisdom to affect a more positive experience with the world around them.

Transactional

Transactional analysis was developed by

Analysis   Eric Berne and is a widely recognized
form of modern psychology. Both client
and therapist engage in a contract that
outlines the desired outcome the client
strives to achieve through therapy. They
then rely on their adult beings to identify
and examine various thoughts,
behaviours and emotions that hinder the
client's ability to thrive. The atmosphere
that supports transactional analysis is
one of comfort, security and respect. A
positive relationship is forged between
the clinician and the client in order to
provide a model for subsequent
relationships that are developed outside
the therapy arena.

F.
Organisations for The Elderly
Useful Links And Addresses

Organisation	Aims	Website	Phone
Age UK	Advice, information and support	www.ageuk.org	Advice line: 0800 169 6565
Alzheimer's Society		www.alzheimers.org.uk	Helpline: 0300 222 11 22 Switchboard: 020 7423 3500
The British Association for Behavioural & Cognitive Psychotherapies	Counselling	www.babcp.com	0161 705 4304
The British Association for Counselling & Psychotherapy	Counselling	www.bacp.co.uk	01455 883300
Citizen's Advice Bureau	Advice and information on your rights including debt and consumer issues, benefits, housing, legal matters.	www.citizensadvice.org.uk	Refer to your local phone directory
Direct.gov	A huge repository of information about public services, the Direct.gov website includes useful information covering various topics such as life episodes, home and community issues, employment, the law and many more.	www.direct.gov.uk	Not available
Friends Of The Elderly	Residential care homes, nursing care homes and dementia care homes; day clubs, home support, home visiting, telephone befriending and grant-giving services	www.fote.org.uk	020 7730 8263

Good Access Guide	The online guide to life, leisure and mobility. The UK's leading directory of services for disabled people, seniors, and anyone whose life is made easier by better access to goods, services and amenities. That's pretty much all of us!	www.goodaccessguide.co.uk	Not available
Independent Age	Independent Age is a national charity providing information to help older people stay independent.	www.independentage.org	Advice line: 0845 262 1863 Switchboard: 020 7605 4200
Retirement Matters	Retirement Matters has a general range of services from health and care to travel and shopping. Designed for the over 50s.	www.retirement-matters.co.uk	01273-749990
Saga	*Saga* offer an array of products and services exclusively for the over 50s, including insurance, home care, holidays and the UK's best selling monthly magazine	www.saga.co.uk	01303 771 111
Saga Connections	A dating site for 50+s	www.sagaconnections.co.uk	Not available
Seniors Network	Seniors Network is an information resource for older people. It encourages all Seniors to take an interest in technology, computers and the Internet.	www.seniorsnetwork.co.uk	01236 435 156
Silver Surfers	A very comprehensive site packed with information on a wide range of	www.silversurfers.net	Not available

	subjects for the over 50's. General knowledge, travel, etc.		
We Are Better Together	For over 50s looking for someone with whom to share their home, holidays, hobbies or heart.	www.wearebettert ogether.co.uk	0871 7810777

About The Author

David Buswell was born in Northampton.

After leaving Uppingham School, he went north to Leeds Polytechnic, and then west as a postgraduate student to Manchester University. Qualified for employment he worked in several financial services organisations before setting up a market research company.

While on a visit to Findhorn he discovered the psychological model of Psychosynthesis. He was so entranced and captivated by this approach, that he did a three year postgraduate diploma in Psychosynthesis counselling with the Psychosynthesis & Education Trust in London, subsequently working as a counsellor. He later trained in Neuro Linguistic Programming, qualifying as a Practitioner and Master Practitioner in NLP. He is a member of the International Coaching Federation.

In 2000, he set up *Virtuoso* Coaching, a consultancy which specialises in helping musicians and performers in general to achieve peak performance and to overcome performance nerves. In 2006 he published *Performance Strategies for Musicians* a self-help manual for those who suffer from stage-fright and / or wish to perform at their very best.

David is a pianist, organist and a choir trainer. He has been organist of several churches in Leeds, Assistant Director of the Bradford Choristers and has taken choirs to sing in a number of UK cathedrals. He has cycled from St. Malo to Montpellier, and round the coast of Scotland from Glasgow to Inverness. Once.

Acknowledgements

My thanks to those who have in their different ways contributed to this book. First, my thanks to Marie de Hennezel for her meditation on ageing, *The Warmth Of The Heart Prevents Your Body From Rusting*, which was one of several stimuli that started me on this journey of discovery. Also to:

Rachel Alexander
Fellow NLP Coach, who has been a wise, positive and bountiful source of advice on the writing of this book. She read the first draft and made many valuable suggestions. Time spent with or talking to Rach is at least as good for my spirit as reading Chapter 7!

Rona Buswell
To whom I owe so much for turning me round and pointing me in the right direction. She opened doors for me into rooms that I did not know existed. I thank her for her unique thinking, and for the example she sets to me and many others of how to live a spiritual life.

Ruth Pimenta
A companion on the Psychosynthesis journey, who, when I said I was thinking about writing a book with the working title of "Amazing Ageing", said without hesitation 'That's fantastic' and has been the personification of encouragement. She read an early draft and made many helpful suggestions. Thoughtful, compassionate and direct, she is a true and wonderful friend.

Riaz Rhemtulla
Another prime candidate for being the living embodiment of the seventh chapter, he has been a great support as this book made its way from an idea buzzing round in my head to becoming something more concrete. As ever, Riaz has been a calm, cheering and cheerful presence; I have learned much from him about living a reflective and contented life.

While I have scrupulously checked the source of quotes and ideas mentioned in this book, if I have failed to acknowledge any source or to give credit where it is due, I apologise and will make good the error in any future editions.

Amazing Ageing

Talks, Workshops & Courses

The message of "Amazing Ageing" is indeed so amazing that we should not keep it to ourselves.

I would be delighted to give a talk to a group or organisation in your area. If this is of interest, please contact me.

If you would like me to run an Amazing Ageing workshop or course, please get in touch.

I can be contacted at **david@amazingageing.co.uk** and, wherever in the world you live, I look forward to meeting you.

Thank you.

Lightning Source UK Ltd.
Milton Keynes UK
UKOW03f0643120814

236789UK00001B/21/P